THE WOMAN

WHO

GAVE BIRTH

TO

HER

MOTHER

ALSO BY KIM CHERNIN

The Obsession

In My Mother's House (Memoir)

The Hungry Self

The Hunger Song (Poetry)

Reinventing Eve

The Flame Bearers (Fiction)

Sex and Other Sacred Games (with Renate Stendhal)

Crossing the Border

A Different Kind of Listening

In My Father's Garden

Cecilia Bartoli: The Passion of Song (with Renate Stendhal)

My Life as a Boy

KIM CHERNIN

THE WOMAN
WHO
GAVE BIRTH
TO
HER
MOTHER

Seven Stages
of Change
in
Women's
Lives

VIKING

VIKING

Published by the Penguin Group
Penguin Putnam Inc., 375 Hudson Street,
New York, New York 10014, U.S.A.
Penguin Books Ltd, 27 Wrights Lane, London W8 5TZ, England
Penguin Books Australia Ltd, Ringwood, Victoria, Australia
Penguin Books Canada Ltd, 10 Alcorn Avenue,
Toronto, Ontario, Canada M4V 3B2
Penguin Books (N.Z.) Ltd, 182–190 Wairau Road,
Auckland 10, New Zealand
Penguin India, 210 Chiranjiv Tower, 43 Nehru Place,
New Delhi, 11009 India

Penguin Books Ltd, Registered Offices:
Harmondsworth, Middlesex, England

First published in 1998 by Viking Penguin,
a member of Penguin Putnam Inc.

1   3   5   7   9   10   8   6   4   2

ISBN 0-670-88096-5

CIP data available

This book is printed on acid-free paper.
∞

Printed in the United States of America
Set in Minion
Designed by Francesca Belanger

FOR LARISSA

Every mother contains her daughter in herself and every daughter her mother, and every woman extends backward into her mother and forward into her daughter.

—CARL JUNG

CONTENTS

INTRODUCTION

$\mathcal{T}$he characters in these stories started out as real people and immediately got disguised. To begin with, names were changed, then physical appearance, places of origin, age, sometimes class and even ethnic and racial backgrounds. As I worked, coded and concealed, I began to realize that an arresting process had been set afoot. The motherly act of protecting a private person from intrusion had brought about an archetypal version of that person, who might still (if so inclined) look back from the text and identify her original, whose identity meanwhile had been concealed from everyone else.

I hoped that in this process true stories about real people would emerge. True stories, however, carried by characters so disguised I had to realize that to some extent they were invented. Clearly, the stories would have to make their way onto the page through the tension of this paradox, filled with characters as authentic as I could make them, yet making it impossible to detect the original people who once lived these tales. I had to preserve the structural core of an emotional situation while thoroughly shielding the identity of the people who had lived it.

As I wrote, I began to think of the people in these stories as transitional characters, who transact their business in a halfway house between the real and the made-up, the remembered and the reconstructed. Sometimes their voices had been carefully re-corded, then disguised; sometimes voices not heard for many years suddenly spoke again in all their original urgency, within my memory.

The Woman Who Gave Birth to Her Mother is the principal archetype we encounter in these pages. She is the most general, all-embracing version of the women who told me their stories, or came to work them out with me. Likewise, she is the principal character with whom, in one form or another, the reader will be asked to identify herself. I think of The Woman Who Gave Birth to Her Mother as every woman (Everywoman) who reaches the particular stage of female development these stories piece together and explore.

The familiar mother-daughter story of our culture tends to be drawn out between the ever-shifting emotional positions of blame and forgiveness. The bad, inadequate, failing, weak, aban-doning mother of childhood is raged at and blamed for every-thing that once went wrong in the daughter's life, and still is going wrong. There are of course daughters who have never been angry at their mothers. Most women, however, know what it means to experience anger followed by a sense of reconciliation and for-giveness. Childhood is reimagined, insight or understanding of the mother's life as a woman is reached, the daughter feels that she has arrived at a resolution of her ongoing struggles with her mother, only to find, in time, that her anger returns, her blaming of the mother starts over again, the two seemingly antithetical emotional positions, blaming and forgiving, turn out to be the twin poles of the mother-daughter story, between which most of us live out our lives.

The Woman Who Gives Birth to Her Mother begins with the breaking of this pattern. It advances into an unexplored emotional territory that is created by a daughter's ability to rework or even shatter what is habitual and limiting between mother and daughter. In this moment, it becomes possible for the daughter to create the mother she feels she has always needed and deserved. She re-creates her real mother or she creates a symbolic mother to hold and foster her psychological and emotional development. That, to begin with, is what I mean by the phrase "to give birth to one's mother."

The first woman who used the phrase in this new and arresting sense had recently contacted her mother after many years of silence, brought her to live with her and painstakingly taught her to become a mother, in a process that closely mirrored the therapeutic work we had been doing. When she said to me, "I have just given birth to my mother," it was the first time, in four years of work, I had heard her laugh, or use language symbolically. To this day she denies that she came up with the phrase and insists that I invented it to describe the process by which she helped her mother learn how to notice, pay attention to, praise, hug, and advise the daughter (now grown up) whom she had never been able to mother as a child.

Teaching the mother to become a mother—this is one sense in which a daughter gives birth to her own mother. It is an act that requires an enormous maturity on the daughter's part, an ability no longer to be bound by the conflicts and disappointments of the past, a recognition that change between mother and daughter is still possible although both the child and the mother of childhood have long since vanished.

Not every mother can be taught to become a mother. There are times when a woman must give birth to her own mother by becoming a mother to herself. A young graduate student told me, during the first months of our work together, that since she had left home to attend college she had never eaten a solid meal she had prepared for herself. She occasionally ate in restaurants, or had a meal cooked by her roommates, but most of the time she ate nothing but sweets, waiting until she felt hungry and then stopping to buy chocolate chip cookies or frozen yogurt. For her to begin feeding herself reasonable meals, which required advance planning, some care for nutrition, an active and sustained concern for her own health and well-being, was a symbolic act of giving birth to herself as her own mother, a necessary step before any further development could take place. I remember vividly the evening I went out to fetch her (she always sat in the garden rather than in the waiting room) and found her eating a substantial health sandwich she had ordered earlier in the day in preparation for our late appointment, which until then had always been followed by a dash down to the nearest Mrs. Fields. She looked up at me with an exhilarated expression, delighted, I thought, that I, having come out a few minutes early, had discovered her in the middle of her first self-arranged, deliberate, solid meal.

Another woman gave birth to her mother by deciding to undertake an unlikely search for her birth mother. I had wondered about this, as it involved the use of her last remaining funds, distracted her (I thought) from the important tasks of finding a job and developing a relationship in the present. My client was a lonely, withdrawn woman, who had attained certification as a masseuse but had never been able to work as a massage therapist because she could not bear to charge her patients. She was now in her late thirties, had never held a job for long, had never had a relationship, was suicidal and depressed. I had thought of this need to spend all her resources on an unlikely search as representing a fixation on the past that was costing her a great deal in the present. She disagreed. She had always felt unhappy in her adoptive family, where she had been severely beaten and punished as a child. She was convinced that she had a mother somewhere in the world who could love and understand her. I thought this was a fantasy and encouraged her to give it up. She paid no attention to me. She felt urgent about finding her mother, who she thought might otherwise die before she ever had a chance to know her. She undertook the investigation on her own, developed intricate and clever means of tracking down possible leads, and after several years of looking made contact with her birth mother, who welcomed her to a family that had always regretted the loss of her. Less than a year later the birth mother died, leaving my client with a very close relationship to a large, boisterous family, half-sisters and brothers, uncles and aunts and grandparents. Her birth mother also left her a substantial sum of money, with which she was able to buy a house and devote herself to establishing a woman's shelter in her community.

In retrospect, I would say it was not merely the finding of her birth mother, but the way my client undertook the search for her that represented the crucial developmental step of giving birth to her own mother. The quest was pursued with her own emerging sense of vision and value, and with her own ingenuity, and in clear opposition to my judgment. She had to follow her own sense of authority for her life although she knew that I had strong doubts.

In this sense, she gave birth to her mother by finding in herself the resources to oppose me and my more conservative, conventional approach to her life.

For the women with whom I have spoken over the years, the idea of giving birth to one's own mother has had many meanings and applications. Part of the fascination of these stories, for me, has been the anticipation of what the phrase can possibly come to mean next—how many meanings and turns can be given to it and how many different applications it can come to have, as each woman comes to understand her life through the concept.

The process of giving birth to one's mother is always a symbolic act, even when it involves a changed relationship to one's actual mother. It is an act that can, therefore, take place whether the mother is living or dead or has ever been known. The symbolic birth begins, as all births must, with a conception: the daughter's awareness of habitual patterns, familiar thoughts, stereotyped and predictable reactions to her mother. The daughter has faced these squarely, and now comes to regret the pattern and hopes to change. The mother who has died, whom one cannot address directly or invite to undertake this transformative work, stays present to the daughter through the frozen pattern of memory and emotion that has come to represent her. If she was, according to the daughter, a mother who failed to recognize her daughter's needs, it is likely that her child will continue to perceive other motherly people as if they were just like her.

A young woman who came to speak with me spent the first six months reproaching me for the way I could not arrange a room that was comfortable, silent, totally private, free from intrusion. Either the room was too hot or cold, there was work going on in the street or the neighbors were using a chain saw or someone happened to knock at the front door, which is next to my office, or the phone rang from a distant part of the house, disrupting the perfect seclusion in which she wished to establish our work. Her mother had died when she was four years old; she had, however, very precise early memories of an anxious, distracted woman, who used to poke her with safety pins while changing her diapers, leave her lying without blankets on a cold day, who yanked T-shirts off over her head, practically "smothering her," and who, she believed, used every opportunity to inflict on her child a hostile, insensitive caretaking. She experienced this same hostility from me in the way I had not managed to make my room soundproof or keep myself from noticing the distracting events that drew my attention away from her, sometimes for a fraction of an instant. I already had the concept of the woman who gave birth to her mother when we began our work. I wondered frequently what it could possibly come to mean for this woman, whether it would apply to her at all and how she would enact this symbolic creation. Our conversations were marked by anger on her part, defensiveness on mine, continual accusations and reproaches from her, which made discussion between us difficult. One day, when she came in late from work, shivering with cold because she had not eaten and had not brought a jacket with her, although she worked outdoors, the characteristic reproaches began about how I was unable to provide a comforting space for her. This time, however, after several minutes of telling me off, she suddenly sat straight up in her chair and said, "Do you have a blanket?" I went upstairs to get her a down quilt, which she accepted somewhat angrily, then carefully wrapped around herself so that only her face was visible. I noticed that a corner of the quilt was brushing against her cheek, close to her eye, so I adjusted it. She nodded her head approvingly and settled back into her chair. "How about a banana?" she asked. I brought the banana. And there I stood, holding it out to her. She didn't move. If she reached out to accept it she would have to unwrap herself from the down quilt. If she stayed wrapped up, she wouldn't be able to eat. She was, I noticed, trying to hide a smile by burying her face in the quilt. Clearly, she perceived only too well the dilemma she had created.

I peeled the banana and offered it to her. I found myself behaving, under the power of this situation she had made, as I might have done with a child too small to feed herself. "Umm," she said, munching greedily and with evident pleasure. She didn't say anything for the rest of our time together, just sat quietly rocking herself in the chair with a contented and prideful expression. No wonder, she had just given birth to me as an appropriate and caring mother. From then on, whenever something was wrong with the atmosphere of my office, she asked me to fix it. She was teaching me how to provide an atmosphere in which she could do her work, free of intrusion and protected from the danger of my real or imagined hostile style of care-taking. The office itself became a safe and comforting maternal environment, another symbolic representative of the mother she was creating. The quilt was always at hand, along with a bowl of fruit, a bottle of water, sometimes a canteen of herbal tea, provided by me. She herself brought in a gadget that made white noise, which she left with me so that we could make use of it whenever the outer world intruded. At first, she was jealously watchful of the white noisemaker and wanted to make sure I did not use it for anyone else. Eventually, she suggested I use it also for other people. Before we finished our work, she began providing the fruit and sometimes brought us coffee drinks from Peet's or even fruit smoothies, which we sipped together as we talked, acts through which she constituted herself as the maternal presence. She never gave up the quilt or offered to make it available to anyone else. When I was away on vacation or out of town for work, I offered to let her take it home with her, but she declined. Apparently, its maternal function was required for this room and our work; the quilt was a prop I had given her, but which she controlled, using it sometimes on summer days when I was sweltering and we had to agree to turn on the fan.

Giving birth to one's mother, whatever form it takes, belongs to a stage when a woman takes responsibility for the relationships and circumstances that will advance her development. Here, the past has begun to release her. What she is becoming matters more than what she has been. If circumstances are not right for her development, she will create them. If her relationships are unsatisfying, she will find or make one good, solid relationship to see her through. Whatever has been seeking movement is ready to move on. It is a breakthrough moment when a pattern is relaxed, a self-authority is assumed, a deliberate act of self-creation is launched, through the establishment of a new relationship to a symbolic mother.

A book too can be a maternal presence, a place from which one seeks refuge, to which one retires to sort things out and take comfort from the act of self-reflection. The characters we find in these pages, real but invented, may stand as close to the reader who identifies with them as they do to the original people from whom these stories were derived. These strange hybrids, these made-up characters who once were real, provide an imaginary space into which readers may freely venture to construct their own version of these stories about mothers and daughters. I imagine readers filling out the margins or the spaces between lines, composing and editing their own similarities and differences to the stories on the page, recognizing themselves, their mothers or daughters, noting important distinctions, wondering whether conflicts, confrontations, confessions, resolutions tried out on these pages might apply to them. What a lovely game for writer and reader, in which the reader may become, through the very act of reading, the Woman Who Gives Birth to Her Mother.

PART I

The
Mother-Story

※

$\mathcal{I}$ listen, on some days for five or six hours, to women of many ages, and for most of that time they talk about their mothers. This does not surprise me or them. They have come to me in hope of healing, and what would healing be if it did not begin and end with talk about our mothers? Sometimes I also talk to strangers, women I run into on the rare occasions I take the bus, women I meet standing in line at the bank or in a supermarket or at the health store. We too, more often than not, have something to say about our mothers. With my friends I speak about my mother or theirs over lunch or coffee, or on long rambles through the city. This is at times the main topic of conversation between us, although my friend Cathy has pointed out that in recent years we have begun to talk, as another way of bonding, as consistently about our daughters. I talk to my daughter about my mother; we talk about me, my daughter's mother, whom she sees in some ways differently than I see myself. Sometimes, when we are taking a hike together, or going about in her neighborhood, in the Mission, I feel that there are two of me—I, myself, and close beside me, wearing the same skin, there is my daughter's mother. One of these days I will have to ask her if she feels herself doubled in the same way, so that when she takes my arm she is simultaneously complete unto herself, while yet her mother's daughter.

My friend Lillian and I have spent more than twenty-five years talking about our mothers, trying to figure out how we are like them and trying hard not to be. Because Lillian was born when her mother was young, and I was born when my mother was aging, our mothers were the same age, although there is enough difference in age between Lillian and me for us to have thought of ourselves, at times, as mother and daughter. A year ago, after all these conversations about the way our mothers were getting old and ceasing to be mothers and becoming more like children for whom we had taken over responsibility, both mothers, both over ninety, died within three months of one another.

My daughter, responding to the death of her grandmother, said, "Now there's only us, Mom," and we both moved up in stature. I became the family matriarch, she took over my place as the family daughter. Now, when we tell stories about my mother, we are talking about someone who lived in the past, and that has come to seem a long time ago.

It has always seemed odd to me that when my daughter tells stories about her mother she is talking about me. My eccentricities and failings are those of a mother who can't quite get things right and has never fully occupied the role of mother and certainly not conventionally. In my daughter's stories, the troubled young woman who left home and went to live somewhere else for many months is a mother; therefore, a mother, some people would say, and my daughter would agree, who abandoned her child. But when I left my daughter with her father I thought of myself as a woman who had to get away from home.

I have heard many stories about mothers who abandoned their children and never thought of myself as The Abandoning Mother, but when my daughter tells her story about her mother, that is the figure I become, at least for a time, before I came back home and tried to mother her again, at which point in her story I may turn into the Young Mother Who Tried Hard and Never Quite Made It, a character with whom it is easier for me to identify. Not that my ease or discomfort should influence the shape of my daughter's stories. They are, over time, sometimes entertaining, sometimes eccentric, sometimes troubled tales, but they are never idle. The stories told about mothers are never idle tales.

Mother-stories have to be told over and over. Repetition is part of their nature. They have come into existence because, like a Chinese box, or a Russian doll, they contain secret drawers, dolls within dolls, stories within stories in a sequence that must be explored, until the heart of the matter, the smallest doll, the innermost drawer of meaning, has been reached. That requires time, patience from the teller and the listener; it requires them to have understood the purpose of a story.

Any story that repeats itself will come to have minor changes, subtle corrections, details swimming up out of nowhere, episodes that had been forgotten or overlooked. Tellers and listeners. They may be friends out on a walk, lovers resting together afterward, strangers at the laundromat waiting for the cherry spots to bleach out on the white pants or professional listeners listening to talkers who have hired them to listen. All, listening carefully, will come under the restless spell of the repetitive story, constantly driven toward its true subject matter, which constantly eludes it.

Mother-stories are told in an effort to relive an obscure past, to tear it out of its distance and force it into the present, where it can be examined with the eyes and understanding of an adult. "I never thought I remembered anything. I didn't think children had a memory. The past was a complete blank. But the minute I

5

started talking about my mom, things started to trickle back and I realized I'd always remembered them, they just didn't seem important, or I didn't know what to make of them, and so they were put somewhere else, like in the back of a drawer. You sort of know they are there and you sort of forget them and that is where your childhood is, folded away until you think you don't have it anymore."

Some stories are told and retold so that the past can be annihilated. The daughter keeps on telling the same old story to keep the past at bay. Her conversation has become an exorcism, driving out anything that might disturb her. The story carries a pronounced tone of insistence, as if someone were about to disagree with her, challenge her, question her version of things. That is one way the listener comes to know that the story is incomplete, is having trouble holding itself together.

"I remember my childhood well. I remember everything about it. I know you think I'm supposed to have forgotten everything important. But I haven't forgotten anything. I remember the way my mother smelled when she got out of the shower, wrapped a towel around her and came to wake me up for school. You never say anything about it directly, but I can tell what you are thinking. You think no mother could have been so perfect. You think there must have been some dust in the corner, somewhere. Something wrong, somewhere. Sorry to disappoint you. My mother and I have been close, like that, since the moment I was born. She says so herself. Everyone says so. Ask anyone; in our case it is really true. We're like sisters, soul mates. My mother says she would die for me and I believe her. Because that is how I have always felt, precisely like that, about her."

Some mother-stories are revenge tales, in which the daughter, the storyteller, has finally assumed power over the past; she can force its secrets into the open, proclaim them in her own words, refuse the silence to which she had been pledged. The intoxication of this newly acquired power works away at the story, causing its repetitions. "She put food on the table, she ironed our clothes, she organized the servants. We had to believe that meant she was a good mother. We all believed it. My sisters still believe it. If you try to come up with any other version, you're out. Forget it. No one wants you. The family spits you out. That's what happened to me. That's okay, I can live with it. Look at the rest of them. Mummies. Wrapped up in the family coffin. I have a tongue, I found my voice, I don't care what it costs me, I'm here to tell the truth."

Mother-stories strike out against change and death, they evoke, crystalize, preserve and restore. In them, the vanished mothers live again, transposed into a mother the daughter can stomach. "It doesn't even sound as if I'm talking about the same woman. Is this my mother? Is that what she was really like? I used to think she was used up, wiped out, a rag. Now I imagine she had found a way to live a secret life of her own, never getting out of bed, letting my oldest sister take care of us. That's the life, this mysterious, inner existence, she has passed on to me. That's how I see it now. But is it true? Is that what really happened? Or do I just keep repeating this idea because it is a more comfortable way for me to describe her absence?"

Some storytellers wrestle with their stories, trying to get free of them, to dislodge their hold on the past; the repetitions in these stories have a desperate edge to them, as if the stories had taken the teller prisoner. "I swore that I would come in here today and say something new. I must be driving you crazy. I keep saying the same things again and again. What's wrong with me? Why can't I stop myself? I'm afraid you'll die of boredom if I go on like this. I know I would. I wouldn't be able to stand it. But it's no use. The minute I walk in the door I remember the way she dropped me off at school on the first day, turned around and walked away. She got into the car without waving good-bye. She left me there. I didn't know when she'd come back. I didn't know if I'd ever see her again. I didn't even know what school was. I thought it was . . . maybe . . . some kind of a prison . . . if I even knew what a prison was back then. Some place they send little girls if they haven't been good. A place they send little girls if their mother can't stand them anymore. I knew I wasn't supposed to cry about it or make a fuss. Everyone else seemed to be doing okay. I thought, If I start acting up they'd think they were right . . . they'd think I was the kind of brat you sentence for life to a place like that. Not that there was anything so terrible about it. It was a normal, ordinary public school. But I could see right away, there were no mothers in that place. There were older women, but they were teachers. A teacher is something completely different, we all knew that. That is why no one protested. That's what I thought back then. We behaved well because otherwise we might never get to see our mothers again."

I heard this story, in virtually identical words, for three months at the beginning of every conversation. These words were delivered with an exaggerated calm, deliberately, slowly and methodically, as if they were being invented right then and had not ever been spoken before, so one had to take care to make sure they came out right. The storyteller seemed to have a meticulous concern with the accuracy of her presentation, as if she wanted to make sure that she got nothing wrong, misrepresented nothing. But in the evening, when I went over my notes, I would hear the words shouting at me from the pages of my notebook; they had become tortured and twisted words, struggling to capture an anguish of separation they represented but could not reach. "I thought I would never see my mother again. I thought that was a place they sent children who misbehaved." But one day the storyteller arrived late, rushed into the room, threw herself into her chair and began sobbing. "The traffic, the traffic," she kept repeating. And finally, "I thought I would never get here, I'd miss my time. I was absolutely terrified I'd never see you again."

On that day the repeating story came to an end. Because it came to an end, other stories were able to take its place. A richness and variety grew up in our conversations, which before had been held captive by the repetitive tale.

"That was how I felt that day at school," the storyteller acknowledges. She doesn't bother to wipe her eyes. "Like that. Just like that. The way I just felt on the freeway in the traffic. Jesus! Poor children! Is it possible? Can a little child really feel that despairing, that desperate?"

The childhood emotion, which had been held at bay by the story itself, now broke through consistently into our conversations. The storyteller began to feel that she was being "given back to herself," or at times that she was "coming back to life." She frequently told me how the world, which she had experienced as gray and static and sullen, was gradually taking on color. One day she walked over to the window, drew back the curtain and offered me the view of the garden. "Is that how it always was? I can't believe it. I must have been half dead, a ghost or something. I mean, were those trees really there? Did I ever see green before?"

$\mathcal{S}$everal years ago I heard a mother-story when I was shopping at the health-food store on Hopkins Street. Back then, I seemed to pick up mother-stories everywhere I went, so that in time I came to feel it was "my duty and my joy," as Oliver Sacks says, "to record and bear witness." In the health store, picking out fruit, and having some trouble deciding on a ripe melon, I encountered a woman who went about things with a brisk, deft air, and I admired her. When she saw me looking at her she immediately came over to give advice and pointed out a couple of melons that later turned out to be delicious. "You should have seen my mother," she said to me, impressively; "my mother could tell a ripe melon from the smell the minute she walked in the door of a market. She didn't have to touch, she didn't have to shake it, she could have picked it out with her eyes closed. Just from the smell and from a block away, I tell you."

I like stories that begin on a dramatic note and evoke the improbable. "I guess she was a great cook," I said.

"My mother? Sure, she could cook. I mean, you wouldn't say she was a great cook. But when she felt like it, sure, she could turn out a meal."

This sounded less enthusiastic about the mother's virtues and made me curious. "Are you a good cook too?" I asked.

"Well, you know," she said, lowering her voice, "my mother never really liked cooking. And I do. So that makes a difference."

I like to cook sometimes and sometimes I hate it. When my daughter was small, during a spell of not liking cooking, I once boiled a couple of hot dogs and served them up to her with pickles and a hot dog bun. Of course, my daughter loved it; but the look she gave me, full of complicity and reproach, secret pleasure and anxiety, let me know she understood that I was cheating and should have been spending time getting wholesome food onto the table.

When I was standing in line at the checkout stand, the woman from the melons caught up with me. She said, "The truth is, I like cooking now. But I didn't like cooking when my kids first came. It wasn't until my daughter was ten or eleven years old and she had a cooking class in school. It was her who liked cooking and so I picked it up from her."

I told her about the hot dogs and the white-bread hot-dog bun. "Hmm, hmm," she said, shaking her head, "you're telling me."

I put the groceries in my car and noticed that I was hungry, so I went back into the health store to get myself a tofu burger. I was sitting outside the store when the woman whose daughter liked to cook came up to me again. I offered her the seat next to me on the small bench, but she remained standing, leaning against her cart. "The truth is," she said, "my mother never wanted to have kids and so we kids didn't have her all that long. By the time I was seven, eight years old, she was off and we never, not one of us, we never saw her again." Here there grew a considerable silence. "But I'll never forget the way that woman could pick a ripe melon," she said.

Then, it seemed, there was nothing more to say; she wheeled off down the street with her groceries and I did not run into her at that store again.

Mother-stories often begin on an idyllic note. If the woman buying fruit in her neighborhood health-food store feels suddenly lonely in the mid-afternoon, surrounded by strangers, her kids off at school and she (well-dressed, wearing a suit) probably on her way home from work, the memory of the ripe melon promises to soothe and settle. Therefore, it will be told again, and perhaps again, and again, to ward off more troubling memories of the mother who was never seen again.

Stories work and fail to work in equal measure; they keep something out while simultaneously they lead on to something the storyteller would prefer to avoid. That is what happened in the health-food store, perhaps because I myself, the casual listener, confessed to being at times a negligent mother; or maybe the melon story had been told too many times and had lost its power to distance and fend off. Or maybe it had never been told before and therefore no one could know what trapdoors and narrative byways it might suddenly reveal.

The sauna is another place women tell stories about their mothers, and sometimes to perfect strangers. I've picked up a lot of mother-stories in the sauna; there, in that sweaty dream state, between cold showers and water over the coals, I've caught up on lots of reasons women talk about their mothers. Sometimes, the mothers are ill or dying or have just died; then the stories strike out against change and death, they evoke, crystallize, preserve and restore. In them, the vanished mothers live again.

A woman I never saw, because I was lying with my eyes closed when she entered the sauna with a friend, told in a whispered voice about her dying mother, who had lost the capacity for speech. Wanting desperately to communicate with her daughter, she had hummed, again and again, a few bars of a melody they used to sing when the daughter was a little girl. "Those were her last words," the daughter said. Later, I heard her humming the melody as she was taking a shower. That night, when I was straightening up around my desk, I found myself repeating, as if it had been intended for me too, this message from a failing mother who wanted her daughter to know that she remembered her.

The sauna preserves a confessional space; the dark, muffled, half-naked bodies of strangers, come to serve as silent witnesses to the intimate, strangely impersonal chronicle of a mother's relationship to her daughter. Some stories I've heard there have been told in the spirit of revenge, the storyteller taking up, through her tale, the power to redress past grievances and wrongs. "I mean, I know what it feels like. I've wanted to pick her up and fling her across the room. But, of course, I didn't. I did not do it. And that's the point. I remembered what my mother did to me and I knew I would never, ever, never repeat that with my own kid."

Someone else in the sauna—I think it may have been the woman stretched out on the shelf below me—mentioned the need to forgive our mothers, a sentiment very popular in Berkeley during those years.

"Forgive her?" the storyteller demanded. I opened my eyes. She was standing up naked next to the coals, dousing them with cold water. Sweat poured over her face, which caught the spectral light from the orange bulb as she tossed the ladle back into the bucket. "Forgive her? Not on your life. If I could restrain myself, if I could hold myself back, she could have too. No. I don't forgive her. I hold her responsible." She walked quickly out of the sauna, pulling the door shut behind her. A moment later, she looked in again. "And I will never, never, never be a woman like my mother," she added as she grabbed her towel from the bench.

"Oh boy, does she have work to do," said the woman who believed in forgiveness.

I went out to take a cold shower. A few minutes later another woman who had been in the sauna looked in on me as I was washing my hair. "You wonder which one of them has the work to do," she commented, about two women neither of us knew.

We two often ended up in the sauna at the same time every day, early in the morning, after we'd had our swim. I don't know if she was there on the day I heard a woman tell her mother-story twice, in almost identical words, before I went swimming and then again afterward. She was telling it to me, but I don't think she realized I was the same woman to whom she had already told it. Her mother had taken her swimming when she was a little girl. They were in a neighborhood pool, in shallow water. But the daughter was scared to death and kept clinging to her mother's neck. She was making a scene, whimpering and fussing, and her mother was annoyed. The other kids her age were doing just fine, splashing and kicking and bobbing their heads. Finally, the mother persuaded her to stand by herself in the shallow water. The mother took a step back. "Just float to me," she said, reaching out her arms so that she could touch her daughter's fingers. "I'm right here. I won't move. I'll catch you."

The daughter floated. She put her head in the water, the way she had been taught, she kicked her feet, she moved forward through the waters of their separation. She lifted her head. Mother was still several inches away. "I'm right here," she repeated.

15

"I won't move. I'll catch you." The daughter tried again, she kicked and moved forward and Mother was still a few inches away. The daughter, who was three, maybe four years old, began to cry. She swallowed a mouthful of water and now she was choking. Mother stared at her with a stormy expression, her arms folded against her chest. "I'm right here," she said again, "I told you I'd catch you." The girl stopped coughing and put her head in the water and kicked her feet.

"That's how I learned to swim," she told me, with a baffled expression. "I was a swimmer all through high school and in college the coach advised me to work out for the Olympic trials. So maybe what she did was a good thing, but I always hated her for it and I never trusted her. It's a long time ago," she said, "but I still don't trust her."

The second time I heard this story, a half hour later, I had the impression the storyteller was trying to shake off the power of this memory, to loosen its hold on her. I wondered if she might tell it again later in the day, if she told it frequently, compulsively, repeatedly over the years, our own ancient mariner of the sauna. The storyteller had repeated not only the words, but had accompanied them with virtually the same gestures and expressions, as if she were evolving her own spell or incantation. Here was a mother-story that hoped to free the daughter from an old tyranny and childhood terror and apparently could not succeed.

I heard another mother-story one day when I was in an elevator with an elderly woman and the elevator got stuck between two floors. "I'm glad it's you," the woman confided in me, "and not some stranger." I didn't have the impression we had met before and asked her if I was mistaken. "Met, not met," she said with an impatient wave of her hand, "you know what I mean. You're not a man, are you?"

I did know what she meant and told her so. I too often feel a sisterly connection with women I have never met before. She punched the emergency button. "You know what happened to me, way back when? I got stuck in an elevator. So I know what I'm talking about."

She punched the button again. A voice came on through the speaker system, asking us if we were okay. "You get us out of here," she demanded.

"So, I'll tell you what happened," she said, turning to me. "I don't know how it happened. But somehow I got into that elevator ahead of my mother. Maybe I ran in, thinking she would follow me. But the doors closed behind me. *Thwock.* I'll never forget it. Such a sound. I heard my mother banging on the doors but it was too late, too late. Oh my god, it's all over, I thought. I'll never see my mother again. So there I am, scared. There's this man there. He looks at me, I look at him. 'Don't worry, girlie,' he says, 'we'll get off at the next floor and your mother will come for you.' Okay, he's right, I'm a reasonable sort of person, I can see that for myself. But the elevator isn't moving. Now I hear my mother's voice, shouting down from the floor above. 'Don't cry,' she's shouting to me, 'don't be afraid. We're coming to get you.' But of course, my mother sounds terrified, just terrified. You know how mothers get? Well, I was her first daughter, back then I was her only child, so you could imagine. Well, to make a long story short. The man turned out to be a good man, that happens. He didn't want to hurt me, he just wanted to help, he pushed the emergency button, he kept telling me not to worry, my mother would be coming to get me. But I in the meantime am listening to my mother's voice and I know there must be some danger somewhere in this situation, which perhaps this man does not see. It never occurs to me that maybe the danger my mother is worried about is this man. Okay, we don't have to make a big thing out of it. Eventually we get off, my mother comes running down the stairs, I take one look at her and I tell you, I tell you, was this my mother? I hardly recognize her. She aged maybe ten years during that half hour. My mother is so upset we have to call a cab. A cab. And in those days who had money for a cab? We call a cab, we're driving home and the whole time I have my arms around my mother and my mother, she is just shaking. You see what I mean? What happened to me in the elevator didn't happen to me. It happened to my mother. . . ."

Once I had heard this story, I was glad that I was not a man and that there was no mother waiting for us on the floor above banging and shouting. As two women, alone together in an elevator, we seemed able to manage things quite well. I told her a story about the time I was in London with my first husband and I went running down the stairs and jumped into the waiting train and the doors closed behind me and the train took off. I didn't have any money with me, I didn't know where I was going, and there he was, standing in the station waving calmly at me with an ironic smile.

"A husband is not a mother," my fellow captive nodded, knowingly. "If a husband loses a wife, so okay. He can always get another. But a mother cannot replace a child, not even with another child. That's what a mother knows when she sees her little girl go off by herself into an elevator. . . ."

Among all the stories I had gathered up over the years, it was the elevator story that returned to me insistently. I had been impressed with this story about the traumatic event that had affected the mother more strongly than the child. I kept thinking about the little girl in the elevator with a strange man. I thought about the little girl in the cab with her arms around her mother. It was a beautiful story, I had thought, about a mother's concern over her child's safety; it held all the real anguish and alarm at small events that make the daily drama of a mother's life. But it was also an ambiguous tale for the way in which the daughter, during that cab ride, had become her mother's comforter. It was the child, after all, who had endured her first separation from her mother in this alarming way. Yet it was the mother who had been in need of comfort.

Maybe the mother who had abandoned her kids after picking out the extravagantly ripe melons had expected one of her children to be able to comfort and take care of her. Then, when she discovered this was not likely to happen, she took off. I never met this woman. I have no idea what story she would tell about her life. It is too late for me to ask the daughter what she thinks of this idea; I know it is only one of many possible explanations. Mothers disappear from our lives, they do it all the time, not just by taking off or dying. Mothers get preoccupied by their own interests and disappear into them. Sometimes (rarely) it is we who make them disappear: We stop thinking about them, we stop taking them seriously, we outgrow them.

The mother who threw her daughter against the wall might have been furious at the little girl because she, the mother, had to take care of her. She may have thought the child owed that caretaking to the mother for having given birth to her. It is possible, of course, that I have begun to hear this version of the mother-story everywhere I look. The story of the dying mother who hummed a child's song for her daughter does not add much to this train of thought. Everyone who is dying becomes a child again. The mother in the swimming pool, tricking her daughter into autonomy and independence, may or may not have been hoping to get the kid to hurry up and grow up and take care of her.

The elevator story told about the way a frightened little girl had become a little mother. Was this an exceptional event or was it typical? Did the mother get so upset every time the child was upset that the daughter had to take care of her? Was this a coded story about an unfortunate reversal of roles between two generations, in which the daughter is (unconsciously) expected to mother her own mother, sacrificing her own needs and perhaps, too, her own capacity for independence?

Is this the story many women had been trying to tell me? That their mothers had given birth to them in the hope of finding a mother for themselves?

I seemed, during those years, to have had the mark of a listener sketched on my forehead. Sometimes an encounter was so slight I had to marvel at the ease with which women began talking about their mothers. Once when I was putting quarters into a parking machine at a lot near the Opera House, a woman came up to put her quarters into the machine. We had, it is true, more than a few seconds, but not more than a few minutes, during which she told me, as we walked back to our cars, how her mother had only learned to drive when she, the daughter, refused to interrupt her own day to pick her up, to take her to appointments. I saw the mother sitting at the steering wheel. She rolled down the window to look out and said, "I'm getting my driving lesson," with an adorable girlish pride that made me appreciate what a struggle it must have been for the daughter to set this task in motion. I can see them to this day, the daughter prematurely gray and stooped; the mother, a woman in her late sixties, leaning coyly against her hand, toying with her blond curls, smiling up at me.

When I was alone, wandering about or involved in my own thoughts, the stories I had gathered in would rise up spontaneously and play through me, a collective choral ode chanted by daughters in homage to their mothers. Sometimes, when I was lonely or sad, they arose in a more intimate vein, ballads of a primordial filial love that could never die. And what, I wondered, were we trying to accomplish through these stories? They held all the essential episodes through which love passes in its fretful journey to completion. There were golden memories, followed by loss and longing, outrage and forgiveness. I had gathered up heated tales of identification and the failure of identification, through which the storytellers seemed to be striving toward an unidentified goal. What were we after? What secret purpose did these stories serve? What were we trying to get at through them?

Perhaps the stories were chapters, fragments, pieces of a larger composition that the daughters were struggling to complete. Maybe what we wanted from our telling and retelling was some larger tale of the relationships between mothers and daughters. Perhaps we had been listening for a hidden theme, something almost there but not quite risen to the surface, and so we told our mother-stories in the hope that one day we would come into the knowledge the stories promised and withheld.

CHAPTER

4

.

"The woman who gave birth to her mother" is a compelling, ambiguous, ever-changing phrase. When I first began to use it to organize the mother-stories I was collecting, I thought it referred to mothers in need of mothering, who gave birth to their daughters in the hope they would receive comfort and care-taking from them.

I used to introduce the phrase lightly when women in my clinical practice were talking about their mothers. "Ah," I might have said, "so she thought she gave birth to her mother when she gave birth to you." Or I might have gone at things a bit more indirectly: "So, your mother always wanted a mother. Then you were born, her first daughter, and she got what she had been looking for."

Sometimes these comments fell wide of the mark, and that made me regret having spoken them. Sometimes the response to these remarks was direct and vivid. "I was my mother's breast. She was constantly sucking off of me and I couldn't stand it. Yuck, disgusting. She gave birth to her own breast. And then she resented me for needing hers." On other occasions, the concept seemed to enter the story and begin to shape it from within. Without apparently having heard or acknowledged the phrase, a daughter telling her story would make use of it as a magnifying glass that brought neglected aspects of a picture into view.

Mother-stories, once liberated from the repetitive tale, launch themselves on a heady revision. Richness, paradox, subtlety and nuance now take the place of the unchanging story. Distinct patterns of storytelling emerge—as if the mother-story were fated to pass through a series of stations, dragging the storyteller along with it.

I can't claim that every woman who talks about her mother is trying to tell the same hidden story; with some storytelling daughters, however, you don't have to guess. The stories seem drawn along a dedicated track, passing through recognizable stations. This is, of course, hardly a linear journey. A storyteller embarked on this train can get on at any station, rush forward, travel backward, leap over a stop or two, find herself right back at the beginning just when she thought the journey had come to an end. But sooner or later, if a woman talks long and hard enough about her mother, characteristic elements of the mother-story begin to appear.

I don't know that I believe in patterns. Most of the time, it seems to me that sequence and stages are imposed upon events, giving them an appearance of order they do not deserve. When I am listening to a woman talk I am not thinking about patterns. The emotion that emerges, her struggle to fend it off, the intrusion of the past, the difficulty telling some things, the onrush of others, make it unlikely that a listener would sense an underlying order. It is late at night, when I am sorting through my notes, that an implicit pattern seems to emerge.

If we construct an abstract sketch of the stages the mother-story covers, it would look and sound something like this:

I: IDEALIZING

We begin, more often than not, with a sunny, whitewashed view of our childhood, the mother idealized, the relationship between mother and child sketched in without much detail, the early years covered by a rosy glow of well-being. If the storyteller remembers anything difficult or disturbing, she is not yet aware that these more somber, isolated events may have had consequences. She can't feel their impact, sees no reason to dwell on them, can't believe there could be any connection between "that old stuff back there" and the dilemmas with which her current life confronts her.

"We Were the Perfect Family. I Never Heard My Parents Say a Harsh Word to One Another. My Brothers Never Fought with One Another and They Were Always Very Respectful of Me. I Was Everyone's Favorite, the Golden-haired Child, the Only Girl, the Youngest. And All This Was Because of My Mother, Who Always Put Her Family First. She Had a Lot of Work, Managing Our Big House, but She Always Had Time for Me. Every Day When I Came Home from School My Mother Was There. I Changed My Clothes, Came Down into the Kitchen and Found a Glass of Milk and a Big Slice of Home-baked Chocolate Cake Waiting for Me on the Table. Then, My Mother Would Teach Me All Sorts of Domestic Things, How to Sew, Knit, Darn, Iron, Even My Father's Dressshirts. I Never Thought of These Things as Work, I Just Thought Mom and I Were Playing Together. There You Have a Perfect Picture of What My Life Was Like. From the Time I Can First Remember, Until My Parents Got Divorced, When I Was Eight. Then Everything Changed; We Never Saw My Father Again, My Mother Had to Take in Boarders, but the Cake and Milk Were Always Waiting for Me on the Table When I Came Home from School."

There is no need to interrogate the idyllic story; told often enough to a listener who manages to stay receptive through its repetitions, one day it loosens its hold, shaken down by its own contradictions and simply falls apart. The teller remembers tensions between Father and Mother, the mother's depressions, grief hidden away by the time Father came home late from work. The cake and milk remain on the table, but the picture of the woman who put them there changes considerably.

II: REVISION

We have moved on, we have left behind the familiar ground of the original story. Suddenly, we see everything in a new light, transformed by a changing perspective. Here stories emerge in which the storyteller suddenly grasps the meaning of events that had been neglected or obscured; she is shaken, she doesn't want to accept her own stories, she shrugs them off but they keep returning. In an effort to defeat the power of the emerging stories, she sometimes decides she is getting nowhere, isn't learning anything about herself, isn't changing, might as well try some other form of work. If she stops telling her story, the past returns to its settled, sunny version. But if she keeps talking, she is likely to meet up with feelings and stories that take her by surprise.

"How do I know I'm not just making it up? One thing's sure. No one in the family would agree with me. If you had them in here, they'd say I was exaggerating. They always thought I was too sensitive. If they heard me now they'd know they were right. Is that what it was like? My father beat my mother? Sometimes her face was so swollen when we came home from school she refused to leave her bedroom. We could hear her in there, sobbing into the pillow. It was my oldest brother who took care of us then. He's gay, and maybe that's the reason. But we all tried. I remember how lonely we felt. Sometimes, I remember just sitting there. Just sitting there at the kitchen table and my brother would tell me to drink my milk or eat a bite of cake and I couldn't, I just couldn't. We never said anything to each other but we all knew, Mom was upstairs in her bedroom and she couldn't face us, she couldn't come out of her room. Then Dad came home and we had to pretend we knew nothing. We had to pretend nothing was happening. Is that what our family was like? Did we live through that? Is that why I sometimes find it hard to get up in the morning and am still so depressed at the end of the day?"

III: BLAMING

Some women start talking about their mothers with a distinct note of outrage and fury. They recall nothing of value from their childhood. For them, the storytelling sequence begins with rage and blame and tries to get stuck there. Any story, any detail or chapter in it, as soon becomes clear, can become the repetitive story that freezes the progression. No matter where the storyteller begins, she has to move on, forward, backward, sometimes in both directions simultaneously, if a full portrait of her childhood is to emerge.

For the daughter who remembers the milk and cake, the progress into anger proves difficult. She has just come to understand the depth of her mother's despair. Now she refuses to add to it a critical view of her mother. This view, she attributes to me, the recipient of her buried anger at her mother.

"I know what you are thinking. You think she should have left my father years before. She was an educated woman, she could have gone back to work, she had a life before we were born. You probably think she would have done all her children a favor by providing an example of a woman's pride instead of letting herself be broken and humiliated. I reject that view! It's the sort of thing you feminists always come up with. You have no sympathy for the ordinary woman. You want all women to be superwomen, and to tell you the truth . . . you make me . . . it makes me . . . kind of angry. I am convinced that my mother did everything she could. Even when my father was still there, she tried to protect us children from knowing what was going on. She would come out of her room, her face covered in makeup, but of course we could see the bruises. What was she supposed to do? Walk out on him? Gather us up and put us in the car and drive us off to Grandma's? My father had the only car in the family, although he sure could have afforded another. My mother used to take me to my ballet classes on the bus. On the bus. And we had two changes. You think I'm going to get angry at a woman like that? You think I'm going to turn against her?"

[GUILT: Guilt cannot be given a set place even in a highly flexible sequence. With a good listener's ear, guilt is readily detected through most phases of storytelling, an undercurrent of anxious, brooding concern about the mother. For that reason, I bracket this element of the mother-story so that it can be considered a thematic thread rather than a chapter or a station. The movement from idealization to revision is often accompanied by guilt; the storyteller feels that she has diminished the stature of her childhood's principal players. The guilt this evokes may cause her to lurch back into an insistent idealization, a return to an earlier chapter that mocks our efforts to establish a legitimate sequence. Similarly, episodes of anger and blaming directed at the mother are likely to be followed by passages of guilty self-reproach, in which the daughter implicates herself in her mother's unhappiness and accuses herself of causing the problems of her childhood. "I always felt we should have done more to help my mother. Maybe if we had spoken up, challenged my father, let him know we knew what was going on, things could have been different. As it was, we just went along with things pretending they weren't happening and maybe because of that my father assumed we were on his side. Why didn't I go into my mother's room when I heard her sobbing? Why did I have to pretend I heard nothing? I could at the very least have comforted her, couldn't I? I was the only other woman in the house. That's the least you could have expected from me."]

IV: FORGIVING

Some women rush into a forgiveness before they have discovered anger. They don't blame the mother, they don't hold her responsible, they are hard on themselves for whatever difficulties they experienced in childhood. Their forgiveness has an insistent, often cloying quality and easily becomes their repetitive story.

"I know that she did her best. What's the use blaming her for something that happened so long ago? She tried, didn't she? And there were all those circumstances I've told you about. Her father had died when she was a kid, her mother never managed to make ends meet. My father took off, leaving her with me and my brothers and no job. To tell you the truth, my heart breaks when I think

29

of it, she wasn't yet thirty years old and her life was over. I'm not going to add any harshness to that, believe me. If I was ever angry at her when I was growing up, and I'm still not so sure that I was . . . although you people always think everyone should be angry at their mothers . . . although I do remember my brothers and me talking—how she ought to leave my father, just get out of there, I remember that, but it was my brothers, mostly my older brother, the one who became gay, he was always talking about getting a job and supporting us and moving out of town, but of course, how could he? We were all terrified of my father. Especially my older brother. Was that her fault? When she tried to stop him beating my brother . . . [a long, astonished silence]. Did I say that? Did I really say that? Is that what I really remember? I mean, he would just turn on her. She couldn't protect us. Not that my dad ever hit me. I mean, after all, I was the golden-haired one, the baby [the story is interrupted by a muffled, bewildered crying, during which the storyteller keeps looking around the room, as if seeking someone who would disconfirm her story] . . . I think she tried to protect me most of all. She tried, but she just couldn't. And I can't hold her responsible for that. If I ever did, I long ago forgave her, didn't I? Why wouldn't I? Any daughter would, I mean, you'd just have to, wouldn't you?"

V: IDENTIFYING

For the daughter who begins with anger, the identification with the mother, with her position as a woman, is often a far more significant accomplishment than forgiveness. The angry daughter has developed a tough skin; forgiveness seems soft and flabby to her, she wants a strenuous, a hard-won reconciliation. She wants to paint the story out on a large canvas, where one can talk meaningfully about the condition of women. For years, as she leaves home and moves away from the family, she does everything in her power to distance herself from an identification with her mother's life. Then, when she marries, or has a child, or loses someone she loves, she begins to think back on her mother's life through a newly awakened sense of identification with the older woman. Her stories pass through gestures of forgiveness and arrive at a comprehensive, often feminist understanding of the mother's life and choices. Now anger is directed at the circumstances of her mother's life, at society, the system, "patriarchy."

For the daughter who finds it difficult to be angry, and is very eager to forgive, the identification with the mother is a more complex matter. She has always seen her mother as humiliated and broken. She has forgiven her for her failure to stand up for herself or the children. Feminism does not attract her; it seems to contain an implicit critique of her mother's failure to be the woman feminists admire. Identification with the mother is dangerous, it suggests that the daughter will share in the mother's lot, be unable to defend herself or her children, fail to make a meaningful life for herself. Identification with the mother becomes possible when stories emerge of the mother's efforts to protect herself or her children. These, of course, have been withheld from the storyteller's repertoire during all those years when she could not allow herself to know how difficult family life was during her childhood. Now, as the milk-and-cake story becomes increasingly irrelevant, the daughter discovers repeated acts of courage and defiance on her mother's part. With these she can now identify, moving with them into a worldview that is tougher, more embracing, more enduring than forgiveness.

"One time, there was one time, it happened late at night, I remember because I heard loud voices and woke up and got out of bed and went into the hall. I think he was chasing her or something. Then he must have spotted me. She pushed him, and he was a big man. She shoved him out of the way and threw her arms around me, I mean I was really little, she had to kneel down or something to put her arms around me, to keep him away, but he just threw himself on both of us, I guess he had been drinking, and she completely covered me, she took all the blows on herself, how could I ever forget it? That's what she did. That's what she did. I mean, he could have killed her. I don't think she'd ever opposed him before. Maybe that was the first time. But she just wouldn't let him get at me. I don't know where my brothers were. Maybe they were away at camp or something. It was just the three of us and it went on and on and on. And it wasn't the only time. God oh god oh god oh god . . ." [The story is interrupted and does not get taken up for many weeks. The storyteller is hunched over her knees, rocking herself. We sit there for a long time after the session has come to an end. I move my chair up close but I don't touch her. After a long time she draws her left foot up next to mine so that I can feel its pressure. I put my hand on her shoulder and the rocking gradually subsides.]

VI: LETTING GO

Releasing oneself from the pattern of attachment and reaction to the mother is a complex process that can be experienced in several phases. It does not mean forgetting, shrugging it off, forgiving or transcending. It does not bring the mother-daughter relationship to an end or even reverse its patterns.

To begin with, it is a difficult position to hold. One day the daughter announces that she's ready to move on, leave it all behind, put the relationship to rest and get on with her life. That night she dreams an anguished dream about abandoning the older woman, running after her train as it pulls out of the station, looking for her all through the city where she grew up. She wakes up in tears, eager, once again, to forgive the mother for all those deeds and misdeeds and imagined transgressions that had already been forgiven long ago. Or she gets angry at the difficulty of making progress, feels bogged down, pulled back to the beginning, gets angry and blames this on the mother. Of course she's responsible for the depression that has just set in, the struggle to finish the thesis, the pending divorce. "I thought I forgave her. I did forgive her. I forgave her a long time ago. But somehow today I can't stop thinking about the ways she always let me down. It bugs me, it really bugs me and I'm fed up with it, I'm fed up with her and me and this whole damn process. . . ." The daughter, who thought she was in an advanced stage of her relationship to her mother, is blaming her again, stuck in that story and can't remember how she closed off this chapter the last time around. Abandoned tales show up again; they get repeated; there is exasperation and frustration; the stories break through finally into some crucial feeling or insight. The stalled train chugs forward again.

Then a relatively long phase, during which things happen as they do, the mother does what she does, the two of them get into their struggles; but now, amazingly, the daughter is no longer so deeply affected. "I used to die, I used to just die whenever she was sad or lonely. My brothers and me, we had our lives, we tried to go see her as often as we could and of course we all sent money to support her. But sometimes I could just hear something in her voice, how sad she was without us, and I'd drop everything to go to her. We always had a regular call. Sunday nights, after the rates went down. The same exact time, year after year. I could never have a whole weekend to myself, I always had to get back for that call, I remember one time in all those years she had to be somewhere, or do something, probably for one of my brothers. And I just went to pieces at six o'clock on Sunday night. I thought I'd never see her again. I just went to pieces, I did, I went to pieces. I kept looking at the phone, it didn't ring, I'm so ashamed, I mean, I wasn't a little girl, I was grown-up, I had my own kid and I knew she wasn't going to call, we'd arranged it like that and my kid kept saying to me, 'It's okay, Mommy, I'll call Gram and tell her you want to talk to her,' and I just saw that we were doing the same thing all over again, here I was, living alone with my kid, there wasn't an abusive husband, but I was coming to pieces just like my mother always did and my kid was witnessing it. Well, I noticed, a month ago or so, one of us called late. I mean, that never happens. Maybe I was the one, I called late, and my mother was just very casual about it. Like she hadn't even noticed. Then another week, I forgot to tell her I wasn't going to be home. She called the next morning to see if I was okay. But it was all very low-key, very casual. I mean, we still call on Sunday at six, but no one falls apart if it doesn't happen, or it happens late, or something else comes up. We still do the same things, but we do them in a kind of different spirit. I mean, not as if somebody's life was at stake. I mean, we're two grown women, I mean, really. It was about time, wasn't it?"

34

Finally, a conspicuous and relatively lasting sense of release. The daughter finds that she has worn out the familiar and trusted mother-stories, can't really inspire herself to tell them again, doesn't see why they once mattered so much. She begins to notice that her mother is a woman living in the present and that this woman may have very little to do with the mother of childhood. A note of bewilderment creeps in as the daughter talks about this mother who has grown old and couldn't really, couldn't possibly be the woman from whom so much was once expected. "One day, I don't know how it happened, but one day I suddenly saw her sitting by the window and I *saw* her, I really saw her, as she is now. Her hair is kind of thin, you know, she has these little brown spots all over her hands and when she picked up her coffee cup I could see that her hands were shaking. Like, well, I don't want to exaggerate, but it wasn't all that easy for her to lift her coffee cup and get it to her lips, you know, without spilling? Wow! I don't know what happened to me. But suddenly it was like I just knew. This woman is a person, she's not just a mother, she has her own life and always has had it with all its problems and this person just can't give what I've always demanded of her. She can't, maybe no one could, it's just not in her, maybe it's not in anyone. Whammo. I let go. I just let go, I mean I stood there looking at her and I released her from the demands I'd always made and then I noticed that somehow I was released too, I'd given up something but I got something in return. There we were, two grown-up women in the dining room, and suddenly I thought, I have to get to know her, and she has to get to know me, because we are something more than I always thought. We are not just a mother and daughter."

35

VII: GIVING BIRTH

If the mother-story is a train that moves through designated stations, it clearly does not take us on a predictable journey. This train, as we have seen, has a cunning way of reversing itself, doubling back, back-tracking, getting stuck, throwing on the emergency brake, slowly getting started again when the track has been cleared. Here, I imagine the daughter stepping off the train, walking out into the station, into a present unburdened from the long shadow cast by the past. Things seem to stand out in bold relief, charged with a conspicuous sense of presence. She breathes a clear, sharp, mountain air—her journey has brought her up high. She will want to pause here for a time to look around her and think back on the great work she has accomplished.

"Everything looks kind of different now, as if I had never seen it before or almost as if the world had just been created. I was coming in here, and I mean how many times have I come in that gate and walked through the garden? So I was coming in here and suddenly everything looked . . . well, it's hard to describe. Have you noticed how beautiful the light is today? A kind of deep autumn on everything? Things look polished, as if somebody had been going about all night buffing them up. I don't know, it sounds silly. But when I got to the door I stood there for a minute and I felt something very odd, as if I was being kept safe, as if there were a kind of . . . maybe a . . . you know . . . sort of a maternal kind of feeling in the garden? Nothing you could see, really. But you felt noticed. You felt as if you mattered. You felt kind of cared for, as if the trees cared and definitely knew you were there. You know, something like that . . ."

The shape of the story she will now tell, about her efforts to give birth to the mother who will watch over and guide her development, cannot be predicted. Few things move directly into their purpose. But sooner or later, if she keeps at her work, she will give birth to the mother she has begun to sense, this symbolic mother she needs to have if she is to give birth to a new self.

She sits down on her pack, puts her elbows on her knees and begins to brood.

Take a deep breath, daughter.

It is easy to slight the power of storytelling. Yet, a good story, told well, contains the dynamic power to bring about the type of developmental change women seek, often in vain, from psychoanalysis and other therapies. There are natural storytellers and women who have never told a story in their lives; both have to tell the mother-story so that it comes fully alive, excavates the past, delivers its transformative potential. A familiarity with the stages just described can help to keep the storyteller on track. It may even be possible, at times, to actively jog oneself forward and go in search of stories it had not occurred to anyone to tell before. I once set myself, during a very angry period at my mother, to remember moments when, as a child, I had been able to identify with her and wanted to be close to her. At first, nothing came. Then, I remembered that I once stole her lipstick out of her drawer in the bathroom and kept it in my room. That reminded me of the time I broke the heel on her best shoes when I tried to trot around in them. I got in trouble because of the lipstick and the shoes but they reminded me that I had once been passionately attached to my mother and wanted to be like her. Now memories started rolling in and I began to keep a notebook of them. The time I accidently backed her car out of the driveway by releasing the brake because I was pretending that I was my mother on her way to work. The time I took her new glasses to school with me because I was planning to show off in them and then, of course, lost them. The memories were filled with the consistent, impish disobedience I engaged in as a child but they also contained revealing signs that, for all my childhood anger at her, I was, even then, trying to be my mother. The memories broke up my anger and made me laugh for a good half hour before I picked up the phone to ask my mother if she remembered these old events that had just become stories. (She didn't.)

Someone else, holed up in a premature forgiveness toward her mother, might do well to try to remember one moment, one single event, however fugitive, when she was angry or frustrated at her mother. I once prodded a friend who was convinced there had been no such angry moments into remembering an occasion when she had stuck her finger into her mother's birthday cake, leaving a conspicuous hole in the top that ruined the yellow sugar rose and smudged the first letter of her mother's name. She never admitted to messing up the cake; the hole had been blamed on her younger brother, "who never got punished for anything." Hmm ... he never got punished for anything? Suddenly, my friend, the storyteller, had been brought back to a childhood outrage about the preferential treatment given to her little brother by her mother.

A good listener is the first requirement for a good story, the ideal fellow-traveler, the companion sitting across from one, stranger or intimate, as the storytelling train starts up out of the station. There is no point embarking on the mother-story until the right listener has been found, coerced, created; or perhaps, in the absence of the right companion, vividly imagined—the secret-sharer of the journal, the ideal dream-reader of the written tale. Stories need listeners who can be there, virtually a part of the story itself, as it unravels. The mother-story especially needs a listener who becomes legitimately puzzled, annoyed, impatient, bored, excited, curious, moved, hot under the collar, as the story draws her in.

A listener requires a suspenseful story, and therefore the storyteller has to provide this tension by moving from the familiar to the less-familiar to what (undoubtedly) was unknown when the storyteller embarked on her tale. When stories are getting stuck, bogged down, becoming repetitive, it is very likely that they have moored themselves in what is already known. Here, the storyteller herself has to wonder what she is avoiding, why she is sticking so close to what she has already said, what she is afraid of in this story.

Of course, some people tell stories in order to silence themselves—to keep themselves from feeling or thinking or talking about more relevant things. A story of this type sounds as if it intends to shout someone down, cover something up, drive something away, and the listener feels immediately bored by it. The storyteller is bored too, but she can't stop talking.

In a good telling of the mother-story, the storyteller has to be constantly looking for her theme, the story's meaning. She has to figure out, from moment to moment, what is at stake, why the story needs to be told, what drives it and eggs her on to tell it. Details are helpful in work of this kind. They invite listener and teller to pay the closest attention to everything that emerges as the story unfolds. By studying the details that show up, often unexpectedly and spontaneously, the storyteller comes to understand that nothing is irrelevant, the smallest objects, the most fleeting gesture, begin to shine with the power of revelation. Memory, after all, picked them up for just this purpose, cherishing this particular detail while thousands of others vanished.

Any story can be smothered in details and lose track of its quest for an underlying meaning. A good listener will prove her worth here by growing restless, wondering what all this is getting at, holding the delicate balance between impatience (too much detail) and fascination (what in the world does this mean?). And of course there are stories so impoverished of concrete moments they cannot come alive; they sketch out an abstract pattern that fails to capture the sound of a voice, the atmosphere of a vanished room. The balanced presence of meaningful detail is a storyteller's best guide to the progress of her venture. I've heard stories that have grown stuck shatter back into life because the storyteller began brooding about a particular detail, wondering why she'd never remembered it before, asking herself what it meant and why it had appeared suddenly in just that place in her narrative.

The storyteller's tale is taken from her life experience and is built upon the authority of that experience. To tell a personal story, one has to believe one's own life is worth exploring, that there is something to be learned or gained from talking about it. There are people who never tell stories, whole families in which the family's past remains unspoken, its patterns, as a family, sensed rather than known and fated more often than not to be repeated. There are people who fear the power of memory to make them feel what they would prefer to have forgotten. Stories, reaching through every possible barrier of forgetting, denial, distortion, substitution, to make their way steadily into the past, take on a threatening and forbidden power. Dull or repetitive or stereotyped stories emerge to take the place of the fiery, dangerous, living tales that have captured the past, or the family itself falls silent and rigorously maintains its refusal to tell until someone starts asking questions, insists upon answers, breaks open the closed territory of the potential story.

The storyteller needs to risk an engagement with recollection, a slippery, uncertain text. The storyteller should be wrestling with memory, with its power to call up, make vivid, actual and present, the emotion, the atmosphere, the feeling-tone that originally accompanied the events now becoming episodes. Memory and recollected emotion—now we are in a position to understand why stories are so powerful. These, its most basic ingredients, are also the prime movers of psychological transformation, as Freud and his followers have made clear.

Women telling stories, and particularly stories about their mothers, are in the possession of a powerful, often unrecognized instrument for their own development. It may be that these homegrown stories are, in certain ways, more successful movers and changers than the stories constructed with the help of a professional listener. The storyteller has got to be wary of anyone who might take over the role of interpreting, organizing or thematically arranging the story. These crucial elements of a story's construction must remain the special privilege of the teller, who has to work her way to them from the raw and often fragmented material of recollection. She must make sure that no listener steals from her the task of finding or imposing meaning on the tale that is changing her even as it emerges. Now that she has remembered this and it has made her cry or rage, another memory suddenly comes to light, with its burden of laughter or outrage, which in turn leads to something else forgotten, which now suddenly suggests a hidden meaning, an insight or understanding that may be elaborated as a thematic structure, through which the storyteller, eyes wide, glistening, a bead of sweat on her upper lip, is shaken out of her usual way of seeing things into a shockingly new take on what once happened. This basically is how psychoanalysis works; this precisely is what we have observed in the woman passing through the stations of the mother-story. This, abundantly, is the potential held out to anyone who starts one day to talk about her mother, stirring up memory and feeling, as the self re-creates and rearranges itself through the emergence of its tales.

Seven stations in the mother-story and each one potentially a stage in a woman's radical transformation of herself. It is through the discovery, reawakening and living out of the mother-story's implicit emotion that we move from narrative into the stages of a psychological progression that will, gradually, liberate the storyteller from an untold past. The mother-story is at its best, and most liberating, when the purpose of telling it is to slip beneath the narrative surface of the tale and make one's way into its subterranean emotion.

Seven stations on the storyteller's journey, seven chapters in the mother-story, seven stages in a woman's psychological development, and yet there is no predictable order, no sense of a linear progression; there is a constant shuttling back and forth between stations, stages, chapters. The act of telling the mother-story becomes an excavation that seeks for lived experience and the lived sense of the past.

Fortunately for the storytellers, the stories that launch this excavation also sustain it; we are working here with the re-creation of the self through the mastery of the art of storytelling, every woman her own Scheherazade, spinning her tales through the thousand and one nights of her effort to understand herself and her relationship to her mother. The struggle for form, shape and meaning through which the stories emerge holds the storyteller when the emotion she encounters threatens to overwhelm her. Through the act of making and telling the story, of consistently finding its verbal and symbolic representations, turbulent emotion is transmuted, its heat and energy now able to be viewed from the protective distance of the narrative itself. It is impossible to overestimate the power of a story simultaneously to deliver emotion and deliver the storyteller from it.

Over time, the story may well teach the teller to be her own listener; with practice, she will be able to note the places the story is getting into trouble, growing thin, falling apart, rushing past certain episodes, choking the narrative with detail. Little by little, the storyteller begins to listen to herself, to see what she is driving at, what the story wants her to understand. This act of listening to oneself talk, paying attention to what emerges from oneself, is an essential part of the transformative power of telling the mother-story and seems to be the spontaneous gift of setting out to tell these stories and sticking with them, wherever they take one.

The seven stories that follow refuse to demonstrate in any orderly fashion the stages, stations and chapters I have outlined. The themes are there, sometimes explicitly present in the narrative, sometimes tucked beneath the surface, where they can be sensed and intuited if not precisely defined. An able reader should have a lot of fun spotting themes as they appear, then organizing thematic elements so that they conform to the sequence I have sketched. This is a good game we are playing, readers and writer together, but should not be taken so seriously that a tale's narrative power breaks under our efforts to make the story fit an abstract pattern. I have resisted the temptation to cramp and schematize these narratives and advise the reader to follow my example, letting the stories speak for themselves as we register their diversity of voices, their free play with theme and variation. In these stories there are no formulas and no set solutions, no secret recipes for resolving the difficulties of being mothers and daughters. Sometimes, the "right answer" for a daughter, the one that leads to "giving birth," involves an explicit break with the older woman, sometimes it is a matter of searching her out, bringing her home and taking care of her. Sometimes the mother is no longer alive, yet the storyteller transforms her relation to her by daring to think a forbidden thought that forever changes the daughter's life. The six stories that follow, as Part II, are all daughter-stories and demonstrate, each in its own fashion, the unruly movement through the complexities of the mother-daughter bond into an actual or narrative moment that can be considered the birth of a mother. Sometimes I identify these moments, sometimes I leave it to the story and the reader to mark out where they fall. The seventh story, Part III, "A Wedding," brings us out onto unexpected ground as a mother takes over the storytelling role to describe the wedding of her oldest child, an event through which, as she and I come to see it, her daughter manages to give birth to her.

PART II

*Six
Stories*

❈

She is, I have written in my notes, a highly articulate woman in her mid-forties. She brings a vividness into the room, a concentrated, emotional intelligence. She is a woman of restrained intensity; she leans forward as she talks, she speaks rapidly. It is exciting to be in the same room with her; she gives the impression that she will come up with something bold and daring. When she is groping through new ideas, trying to sort them out and make them articulate, her eyes comb the ceiling restlessly. Then, when she has found the focus of her thought, she looks directly at me, with a piercing, fiery expression.

WHAT BRETT SAID

My mother suffered from clinical depression her whole life, very seriously. She made many suicide attempts, she had electric shock therapy, and she had severe postpartum depression after my two brothers were born and even more seriously after I was. Her mother also had severe postpartum depression. In my grandmother's case, it was so bad she had to be institutionalized. She was institutionalized immediately after my mother's birth. And so my mother never knew her. My grandmother killed herself in the institution. But once, when my mother was growing up, she asked the foster family with whom she was living to take her to see her mother. They went to the institution, my mother went into her mother's room and her mother said: "I do not have a daughter." Soon after that my mother's mother committed suicide, so that was the only time my mother met her.

What effect did all this have on me? I spent the better part of my adult life until I had children taking care of my mother. Half taking care of her, half blaming her for never taking care of me. I learned, as an adult, not to go to my mother to get my emotional needs met. Most of the time she would get so frantic about my difficulties that she couldn't help me. I'd be crying, so she'd start crying. Once, after my boyfriend had just broken up with me, and I was really depressed, just devastated, I reached out for her. Of course she knew how bad I felt to lose this guy I really loved. But she couldn't help me. She started to feel as bad as I did, just as depressed, just as devastated. I mean, she canceled her whole weekend to spend time with me but she ended up in even worse shape than I was in. She loved me, I know she loved me, but she couldn't help. My own development was squelched so that I could help take care of her. I had to. Who else could do it? My brothers had their own life. My father was busy. I had to take care of her because she was often suicidal.

I can tell you, for my entire life, every time my mother ever talked about her depressions or her suicide attempts or her shock treatments, I would get this clutching of my heart and I couldn't breathe. When I was a child I thought I shouldn't complain because my parents both had such difficult childhoods. My father's mother died when he was a little boy, his father left him with his own sister and my father rarely saw him again. I always thought I had nothing to complain about because both my parents were there and their childhoods had been so much worse.

So I did what kids do if they have to survive. I pretended that a lot of things were good, although they weren't. I was a very forgiving kid. Somebody who grows up with a depressed mother has to be. When I was nine years old my school class was going on an outing. I got so excited I woke up before it was light, way way before I had to get ready. I ran into my parents' bedroom and started tugging at my mother to get up. She woke up and pushed me away so hard I fell and hit my head against the side of the bed. My father had to rush me to the hospital for stitches. When I got home, my aunt was there and she was yelling at my mother and my mother was crying and I felt so sorry for her I forgot myself completely. I just forgot about myself and went over to comfort my mother. I was a caretaker and I wanted to make everyone happy. My brothers and I used to have dinner at five-thirty. My father would come home from work about seven. Every night my mother would scream at him for being late, which he wasn't. She'd lock herself in her room and I would sit at the table and listen to him talk about his day. Sometimes I ate a whole other dinner just so I could keep him company.

I had my first serious depression when I went away to summer camp for the first time, as an adolescent. I was sent to camp because there was some kind of trouble in the family, my mother had a serious depression and had to have shock treatments. I came home at the end of the summer to find that my mother was in love with another man. She wanted to leave my father. He was sick, they were selling the house, she had given away all my childhood toys, or thrown them out, and she didn't have any time for me. She wanted to spend all her time with her new boyfriend. Finally, after weeks of this, we went out to a neighborhood coffee shop and I said, "I hate you. You're not a good mother, you've never been a good mother and I hate you." I knew she thought she didn't get the mothering she needed. I knew she was terribly disappointed by her own mother. She felt that she was doomed from the very beginning, with a mother who disappeared the minute she was born and never recognized her. She was a survivor, but she was a fragile person. Now she was trying to tell me that she didn't get the mothering she needed as a child, that she didn't have a childhood, and that she needed to get some of that right now with her boyfriend. She said, "I'm sorry," and I could tell she really felt badly, "but that's life. You need me and I need my boyfriend and that's how it is." And I said, "I hate you."

Well, I needed her then. And she just couldn't be there. And I couldn't pretend it was all right. I hated her and I blamed her and I couldn't forgive her. I kept thinking, Why wasn't she there for me? Why couldn't she pick me up? Why does everything always have to be about her? Why was she always screaming? Sometimes she got angry and she hit me. I thought she hated me. I couldn't understand why she would do those terrible things to her own daughter. That's not how she treated my brothers. That's not how she yelled or shouted at my father.

All my life the thing I was most afraid of was that I would turn into my mother. I didn't want to get married, I didn't want to have children. My mother always talked about a depression gene, as if I was doomed to be just like her, and like her mother. I used to talk to my father about this. "Well," he said, "you don't have to worry. You've already surpassed your mother." That was his comment, supportive of me, accusing of her. But he never divorced her. Somehow they just survived her affair and went on.

So that was the story. To be like her was bad, not to be like her was good. Of course they had lots of trouble in their marriage because of her depressions and I could see how my father suffered from them. So, I prided myself on not being like her. I went to live in Europe, I went to graduate school in Paris, I became fluent in languages. Everything I did I measured against not being like my mother. That is why I waited so long to get married and have a child. But I must have convinced myself I was out of danger, I was so different from my mother that I didn't have to fear the same thing happening to me. Was I wrong. . . .

I was over forty when I got pregnant. I thought I would give my kid the childhood I didn't have. I thought I would be a mother like my best friend. She was totally connected to her kid, she had been waiting forever for the baby and was happy the way you are when you find a lover. I used to think I would sit in the rocking chair, breast-feeding and singing lullabies. I imagined taking my kid to my friends' houses and going out to lunch with friends and showing off in the park with this really happy and beautiful kid. But I started to get depressed during my last trimester. Pregnancy totally humbled me. I was this strong, successful, independent woman who had defined myself as apart from my mother for my entire life and all of a sudden I was pregnant and sick and I was scared to death, because I must have known what was going to happen. The birth was difficult. I was in labor for over thirty hours. A few days later, after I got home, I noticed that I was really depressed. I'd been depressed before but it was nothing like this. This was really excessive. I couldn't sleep. I couldn't eat. I lost all of the weight from my pregnancy in three weeks. All I wanted to do was cry all the time. I felt terrible about the baby. I couldn't take care of her. I wanted to kill myself. I just wanted to die.

It was one of those times when my husband, who was always very helpful and caring, just couldn't alleviate what I was going through. I cried even more when he tried to help. He was so loving that I felt even worse. Nothing he did could do any good. There was nothing missing in my life, I had everything and nothing could help me.

The worst thing, the very worst thing had happened. I had given birth to a child and I had become just like my mother. I called my doctor every day. He was very careful, really monitoring me. I talked to him for an hour and a half every week and the rest of the time I had to deal with myself. I was completely incapacitated, I wanted to die. There I was, the baby was five or six weeks old, I kept asking the doctor what we would do if the medication didn't work. He said he would have to hospitalize me. I freaked out. There was that mother line of institutionalization and now it was catching up with me. I sat there and burst into tears. Then I was frozen. I didn't know what to do. Finally, I picked up the phone and called my mother. She said, "No one wants to send you to the hospital, but it's not the worst thing in the world. The baby will be in the room with you. You'll get through this and I'll help you. We'll manage."

She began to come over three times a week, not to see the baby but to have lunch with me. We would go out to this coffee shop in the neighborhood and I would be crying. And I would say to her, like you do when you're a child and you're really sick, "Mommy, am I going to get better? Is this ever going to get better? What can I do? I can't stand it."

She would reassure me. She said, "I've been through it, it's awful, but I'm telling you, if I can get better, you can." She held my hand and I believed her, because she really knew. She'd been through it herself. I couldn't believe anyone else. I thought they were just trying to make me feel better, and that made me feel worse. She would say really simple things to me and they were exactly right. Nobody else knew how to say them. I would sit with her at those lunches and tell her I just couldn't stand it. And she'd say, "Listen, you got up, you got dressed, you walked out the door, you sat down, you're eating lunch with me." It was Easter and the last thing I wanted to do was go shopping for Easter presents. But my mother insisted. Our bond has always been expressed through shopping. So she forced me to go shopping with her and to buy presents for everyone. I tried on a hat. And she said, "You see, a week ago you wouldn't have tried on a hat and now you have. So you are getting better."

She kept telling me I would get better and I believed her because she knew. I really think I wouldn't have made it without her. I needed her and she gave herself over to me one hundred percent. Before this, whenever I told her how bad something was she would just get depressed and then I would end up taking care of her, like the time my boyfriend broke up with me. But this time I let her know everything that was happening and she rose to the occasion the way nobody else could. It was her honesty. Everyone else would say, "You're fine, you're fine," but she knew I wasn't fine. In the middle of all this she and her boyfriend had planned to go to California. I just lost it. I told her I didn't know if I could survive with her gone. So we made plans. I would come down for a couple of weeks and, meanwhile, we would talk on the phone every night. So that's what we did. I called her every night and she was there. Most of the time, all I had to say to her was, "This is terrible." You know how it is. It doesn't get better. The longer it lasts, the worse it becomes because you are convinced you will never get better. It was just ten weeks of sheer hell and everyone else was sick of it but she was not. Maybe it was good for her that she went on vacation, that might have helped her keep going. But she never told me if it was hard for her, she didn't complain, she didn't get depressed, she just took care of me.

I don't know why she was able to come through. I don't know why. Maybe it was because the worst had happened, this thing, this depression she had been worrying all her life would happen to her daughter had finally happened. So now she didn't have to worry about it anymore, she just had to help me get through it. Before that, I had always been like my father, outgoing, self-confident, determined, ambitious. I liked being out in the world. I was all the things my mother wasn't. But now that I was in this depression she saw that I was like her but still enough like my father that she could imagine I would get through it. And of course there was also now this third person, this baby we had to take care of. She made it clear that we had to take care of her, we both had an obligation to save her and we did, together we saved her. I don't know why it turned out like this. Maybe she saw a chance to make up for what had gone wrong during my childhood. She was a grandmother now and not the mother of a baby who needed her desperately and she could just suddenly come through the way she must have wanted to all my life. I don't know why. When I picked up the phone to ask for her help maybe that was the first time I'd ever really opened up to her. Maybe that was the first time I didn't try to prove how I was not like her. I just let myself go and she responded.

After about ten weeks the depression started to lift, I started to feel better, and you know what happened? I found that during this depression I had forgiven her.

But it was more than forgiveness. And in some ways I didn't forgive her. There are things she did to me when I was a child that were really terrible. I think she was crazy to do them. I don't have a rosy picture of my childhood. I don't have a rosy picture of the way my mother was with me. There are still the unforgivable things she did to me, and those don't change.

But something happened. Suddenly, I didn't see why I had a right to blame her for my childhood. I said to her, "I can't believe you had to go through this too. I can't imagine how you went through it. I understand the way you were. I wouldn't have made it through this without you." Suddenly I understood her whole life. She never had a mother. She gave birth to this sensitive, psychologically sophisticated child who was capable of taking care of her emotionally, so that's the pattern we fell into. A depressed person cannot take care of a child. They simply cannot do that. I couldn't take care of my daughter during those weeks. We had a nanny, my husband was there, and I felt very bad about it but I just couldn't take care of her. And my mother would say, "Look, she's surviving, she is a happy child, she has other people to take care of her, and you'll get better. You can't do anything about it now. You have to take care of yourself."

So now I understood. That's what she tried to tell me all those years, but I never believed her because my depressions had never been that bad. I always thought, If you just muster up, if you get yourself in hand, you can do what you have to do. But it's not true. During those weeks I just cared about nobody, and that was how she had felt when I was born. I fed my daughter and I rocked her but I was just miserable. They were mechanical things. I thought I had ruined my child. But my mother reassured me and I could believe her, because here she was helping me, and I thought, She's made it up to me, she's mothering me and babying me and childhood isn't the only chance you get to be a mother to your child.

I had been forced into a position where I had two choices. The one was to continue to blame her, and just doom myself and my daughter to the same pattern that had been there for generations. Or I could look at things in a different way. That's why I don't call it forgiveness. I just started to look at things in a different way.

So that was the irony. My worst fear had come true. I had given birth to a child and had turned into my mother. But now, because I knew exactly what she had gone through when I was born, I understood her. Until then, I always thought I would be a mother so completely unlike my mother that you can't imagine it. When I found out I couldn't do it, I couldn't even try, I saw that she couldn't have done it either. I always refused to see things from her point of view. Well, I thought, she won't see it from mine either. But now I started thinking, Oh my god. She felt like this? This is what she went through? And she had three kids at home? And she didn't have a mother? And she was not working, she was living in the suburbs, and oh my god, I can't believe she didn't go into the kitchen and kill herself.

Then I saw something else. I mean, it isn't easy for any woman to become a mother. It's not just a question of depressions and postpartum problems. I started to see how incredibly difficult motherhood is for anyone. For years, I had tried to say that women in her generation married too young and didn't have the opportunity to explore their own lives. That she wasn't able to mother because she had her kids too young. And then I realized, It's bullshit. You're always too young when you have a child. It doesn't matter. You never know what to do. No one's prepared to give up autonomy and independence and selfishness.

I understood why she had always talked about killing herself. I used to think it was selfish and mean. I took it as a personal affront when she would say to me, "The only reason I didn't kill myself was because of you and your brothers." And I would say to her, "That's ridiculous. I don't want to hear that. It's an impossible burden. I can't spend my whole life taking care of you." But now I understand why she had to tell me. She wasn't trying to threaten me. She needed me to help her, she didn't have anyone else. There are no right or wrong things under these circumstances. She needed someone to know how severely badly she felt, just like I needed her to know how severely badly I was feeling.

Then I understood a lot more about how difficult it is to raise a child, how no one is ever perfect, and there are always wounds and there are always things that we do wrong and that's life. If I had to forgive myself for not being a good mother to my daughter when she was born, there was no way I could hold a grudge against my mother.

When I started feeling better I went back to my past. There's this picture of my mother and her close friend who was always there when I was growing up. I always had the impression it was her friend who raised me. In the picture her friend is standing up and I'm on my mother's lap. Her friend is looking at me lovingly, the way a mother would. My mother is looking straight at the camera. She is a very beautiful woman. She was even more beautiful then. I always showed this picture to my friends as an example of my mother's involvement with herself, because she was looking at the camera and not at me. But now when I looked at the picture I suddenly noticed, for the first time, she has her arms around me! I'm standing on her lap and she has her arms around me! It was the same picture, nothing in it had changed, only the way I was seeing it.

I always thought someone else was the good parent in my childhood. My father or my mother's friend. But now I started to remember things my mother had done that I had never thought about. Every night when I couldn't sleep, which was every night for about ten years, my mother would come into my room and do a relaxation exercise with me. She must have never slept. And I conveniently forgot that. She used to bake bread with me. She liked to read to me from Shakespeare and we acted out the parts. These memories didn't change the memories of the other terrible things she'd done, but they made everything more complicated.

Before, when she would say, "I'm sorry I wasn't there for you when you were growing up," I would think, Fuck you. You weren't there, don't even apologize. All you want me to do now is comfort you and tell you I'm okay.

But now, as I started to get better, and she told me again that she was sorry about my childhood, I thought, Well, let's just take it like she means it. She means it. She really means it. And I said, not "I forgive you," but "I believe you." That's what I said. "I believe you."

I knew what it was like to be a woman, I knew what is was like to be a mother, I knew what it was like to be depressed. And now that I had gone through what she had gone through, I was able finally to believe her. Because she should have been believed. And now I did.

CHAPTER 7

SYLVIA'S STORY

She would like to speak with me, she tells me over the telephone, because she wants to understand why people choose to stay alive. She repeats this confusion during her first appointment. She is puzzled and can't make sense of the fact so many people, including herself, day after day, choose to go on living.

"I have the impression you've thought about this a lot."

"Oh yes, a great deal. I believe it may have become a question of habit. Or perhaps one does not feel sufficiently involved in life to make an end to it? If, fundamentally, there is no good reason to go on living, there may also be no reason not to?"

I have also wondered about living and dying and decide to tell her. "When I used to ask myself this question it was because I felt great anguish. I didn't know how I was going to survive it."

"Anguish?" She seems puzzled.

"When I was young I was very unhappy," I explain. "I didn't know how to go on."

"Whereas I," she says, as if stating an obvious fact, "do not know whether I am unhappy or not."

Perhaps she is not asking me why one goes on living. Perhaps she wants to learn how to live. Or maybe even how to come to life. Suddenly, I imagine her life as a long, gray road coming from nowhere, leading to nothing. I do not know what has given me this impression but it is confirmed as our work proceeds. Often, I have a sense of her standing quietly at a train window, looking out at life as it passes her by. When I tell her this she seems impressed. "Yes, you could say, life is passing me by."

When I have something to say she looks up at me with a slight tilt of her head, as if politeness makes it necessary to acknowledge me, although she would prefer not to meet my eyes. I have asked her about this and she agrees. It is hard for her to look at me. Most of the time, she sits with her hands in her lap, her head lowered, rarely lifting it when she speaks. Shoes, bag, skirt and blouse (an invariable costume) always come in matching, muted colors, greenish grays, beige, as if she had made deliberate efforts to make herself as nondescript as possible. Or perhaps, a more troubling thought, it has not required an effort.

Why do people go on living?

We discuss this question for several weeks. Her ideas are highly abstract, delivered in a thoughtful, controlled, consistently soft and somewhat hesitant voice, as if she has to make a great effort to force herself to speak. She believes in God and thinks that it would be a rejection of His gift of life to "cast it off" before its time. Life, she thinks, is given once only and is meant to be cherished. She faults herself for being unable to do so. She imagines life is given for a reason; perhaps so that those who are possessed of it can offer a meaningful service. She does not feel that she has anything to offer. This, however, strikes her as yet another slight of God's gift. If life is to be cherished, if it has been given so that one can offer service, the capacity to do so must be given as well. And therefore, she must be at fault for having been unable to discover it.

She is curious about the reasons I found to go on living and so

I tell her some of them. I hadn't wanted to inflict a terrible loss on my daughter. I wanted, in spite of everything else, to know what she would be like as she grew up. I hoped something might come of all the turmoil and trouble I was experiencing. I too thought we were put down here to offer some kind of service. I thought perhaps the service I could offer would come from having survived the wish to die.

"These are good reasons," she says. "They are better than my reasons. Perhaps, someday, I will come to have reasons like yours, too."

Over time, she tells me her story. Her mother was "taken away" when she was four or five years old. She is not sure of the exact date. She lived with her father, who traveled. She wasn't sure exactly what he did, he never spoke of it. She had no memory of her mother, her father never mentioned her. Her father's sister stayed sometimes when her father was gone, or a neighbor whose husband had left her. As she got older, she preferred to stay alone and her father permitted this. She had always been an exemplary, quiet, demure child, old beyond her years, always doing what was expected of her. She never dated, had no close friends; in high school she had one friend who was an exchange student from Holland and therefore left after a year. They still corresponded and she planned to travel to Holland "some day" to visit her. She has worked for ten years as an executive secretary to a demanding boss who pays a high salary and supervises her closely.

She tells me that someone at her office had been reading a book of mine some years ago. It was a book I had written about my mother. She borrowed it; it made an impression on her because I too, she had noticed, lost someone when I was very young. She wasn't sure, but she thought the loss of her mother might have something to do with the way she was. Not depressed exactly, not despairing; no, that wasn't it.

She looks at me, briefly, hopelessly.

I observe how difficult it is to put words to what one is feeling.

Yes, she agrees, it is very difficult. But she is determined to try.

I imagine that she hasn't had much practice.

She agrees. When her father was at home they always ate in silence. After dinner, he was shut away with his books. She doesn't remember conversations with his sister or the woman next door, although the woman liked to talk and she, a young girl who didn't understand much, would like to listen. She liked the sounds of the words, the way the voice rose up and fell and moved on, but she herself rarely said anything.

I often have the impression, even when she is speaking, that she is not in the room with me. It seems, although I can see her clearly, that she has slipped away, gone off into a space of her own, from which I am excluded. At other times, she reminds me of a bird that has fallen from its nest. Her body is there, but it is uninhabited. That explains her neatness, perhaps. For the first few months, after we have exhausted, for now, the reasons one chooses to stay alive, we mainly sit together. She observes the changing light in the room when the wind blows and the trees cover the skylights. But she seems to be observing these things from far away, trying to convince herself or me that she is really present. Words like loneliness, desolation, bleakness come to my mind when I try to characterize the atmosphere that fills the room as we sit together. Sometimes, when we have been silent for a long time, this atmosphere is difficult to endure and I have to remind myself that she is managing, without words, entirely through her silence, to communicate her condition to me—indeed to inflict it on me, so that I can know it.

Six months, ten months pass and she is still often silent. She tells me about people she has observed at work—laughing as they have lunch together. She wonders what they find to laugh at. She goes to the library after work but sometimes is distracted from her books as she watches people around her. She has seen someone cry as she was reading. She can't imagine what this would be like. Two little girls come in together on Fridays. They are always whispering and giggling. People shush them and stare at them. They don't seem intimidated and this impresses her. "One glance from my father was enough for me," she says. "I would never have dared."

"Dare laugh? Dare giggle? Dare whisper?"

"Dared anything. My father didn't want me to be there. I knew that. I tried to take up as little space as possible. That is, perhaps, why I'm so small."

I smile, but she doesn't. I have never seen her smile. A smile might seem to her too violent a self-expression. Certainly, she is small, the size of a twelve-year-old girl, an immaculate, faded, almost invisible preadolescent who has succeeded in never calling attention to herself. Her life, too, has the shape of a child's structured, carefully supervised existence. She rises early, eats a simple breakfast of poached egg and toast, has a cup of coffee in the canteen at work, takes lunch for half an hour at 12:30, usually eats alone, walks home by herself, stops at the neighborhood market to purchase her dinner, reads after dinner until she retires, early. Sometimes she goes to the library after work. She sleeps well, doesn't remember dreaming, spends the weekends catching up on work (her boss is fair, he pays her for overtime), goes to the library, sometimes takes in a movie. Her only "indulgence" is a fascination with the daytime soaps, which she tapes so that she can watch them later, usually on weekends. She reads *People* magazine and a magazine about royalty and *Life* magazine because, she imagines, reading them has been part of her effort to figure out why people stay alive. Every other Thursday evening she writes to her friend in Holland, who is married now and has three children. Her friend would like her to visit but she has hesitated so far.

She is often lost for words. Although she speaks properly, in a painfully correct English, in a well-bred accent, she gives the impression that words are alien, that she struggles to attach them to her experience but doesn't believe that she succeeds. Whenever she seems very uneasy about this, I talk. I tell her about my sister, since our childhood loss is one of the few things we have, so far, in common. During those times she seems to settle gingerly back into her body, as if she were timidly experimenting with inhabiting herself in someone else's presence. There is a very slight flush to her cheeks, which are usually pale. Her hands, usually motionless in her lap, gesture occasionally. I tell her about the sled my sister and I used to have, which disappeared after her death. I went down to look for it in the basement of our apartment house, but it wasn't there. I tell her that I was very, very upset by the loss of the sled, although I never remember being upset about my sister's death, which no one ever mentioned.

"No," she says, with the very slightest, forlorn shake of her head, "they don't much, do they?"

"Don't talk about people who have died?"

"Once people are gone, they're gone. They've vanished. You know they are there. But no one speaks of them."

I ask her if she ever cried as a child. She thinks it over, feels that she probably didn't. She isn't really sure what crying is. She's seen tears in people's eyes, the woman in the library, for example. She's noticed that their shoulders shake, but she doesn't know why.

"You don't know what they are feeling? Sad, lonely, full of grief, missing someone?"

She repeats the words cautiously. "Sad. Lonely. Missing someone."

The words, when she says them, carry no meaning, they have no inflection, they might as well be sounds in a language she doesn't know.

But I am close to tears. The tears she does not know how to weep seem to have taken up a refuge in me. I tell her about them. She looks at me, curiously, with that odd tilt to her head. "Because you feel . . . sad? Lonely?" But the words still don't seem to mean very much.

"I was thinking I might have been feeling your sadness, which you perhaps don't know how to feel, since no one ever wanted you to feel anything."

She considers this for a long time. Her gaze rises from her lap and drifts with an unsettled momentum across the ceiling. Her fingers, lightly clasped a moment ago, separate themselves and flutter lightly, as if they might have wished to free themselves from her hand. It is the only sign of tension I have ever seen in her. For a moment, a single, breathtaking instant, I feel that she is in the room with me. But a moment later she has vanished, the feelings that might have been hers take themselves off and the room fills with emptiness again, a nearly unbearable sense of desolation.

I never ask myself what I can do for this woman, although our work certainly does not take a conventional form. I know that it is hard for her to come to speak with me, just as it is often hard for me to sit quietly in the room with her. It seems to me that we are both accomplishing something by living through the states she does not know she is feeling because she has never put them into words, or heard them described by anyone else. I do not think it matters much who feels these states, as long as they are felt and little by little acknowledged. Over time, I manage to name sadness, sorrow, feeling lost, missing someone, not knowing what to do, going on somehow. It is heartbreaking to watch her cautiously try out these words, the way someone would pick up, hold to the light, turn over an object she had never seen before. We go on like this, naming silence, for about two years.

Then, one day, I see her in the café where I meet with a friend on Thursday afternoons. I am early, he hasn't arrived yet, I stop at her table to say hello to her. She is holding a cup of tea, gazing down at a book she does not seem to be reading and I have startled her. The cup shakes violently, the tea spills on the page, she makes a sudden, frightened movement, shoving the book aside, but this only manages to further upset the teacup. She gets up, leaves the book on the table, goes quickly out of the café without looking back. I hand the book to the man behind the counter, asking him to hold on to it for her.

By the time I reach home there are several messages from her. At first, I don't recognize her voice. It is agitated, louder than I have ever heard it. In the first message, without saying her name, she asks, "What happened? Can you tell me what happened?" The next message is an apology for having left the first message. The third message, left after an interval, during which calls from other people have come in, begins more calmly. "I would appreciate it if you could call me before our next appointment together. I am . . . I think I am . . . I think you would say I am . . . frightened." Her voice, when it pronounces the word "frightened," begins to tremble. Only with difficulty can I make out what she is trying to say. Then it occurs to me. She is frightened. She has said she is frightened. She is feeling something and knows what she is feeling and has called to let me know that she knows. Because she knows what she is feeling, she can ask for help. This is the first time in two years she has ever contacted me between sessions.

When we speak, that evening, she is very upset. She speaks in fragments, gets exasperated, cuts herself off. Finally, she says, in a clear voice that must have required an incredible effort of self-control, "You recognized me."

"Of course. Why wouldn't I?"

"You didn't before."

"Before? In the café? You've been there before when I've been there?"

"I've always had the idea that you looked right at me, but couldn't see me. I knew you would see me if you could, but I thought I was probably just not visible. I have always had the idea that I could not be seen. I am confused. What has happened that you could see me now?"

"I don't know what has happened. Do you have any idea?"

"I never thought my mother could see me. She would look at me, but she would look right through me, as if I were not there. I remember that. And I remember her standing at the window. Do you remember when you said that I was standing at the train window? I don't think that was me. I think it was my mother."

"You remember your mother," I say with considerable feeling. "I can't wait to hear about her."

"Well, I've taken enough of your time. Whatever has happened I suppose we will just have to live with it."

"I think I know what has happened. I have recognized you and that has helped you to remember the way your mother didn't."

"Well, let's go on next time," she says, as if she urgently has got to get off the phone and can only do it by imitating the way I sometimes end our conversations.

The next time I see her, a few days later, she is dressed in the familiar outfit of skirt and silk blouse, with matching shoes and bag. She is also wearing something new, or something I have not seen before. I admire it from a distance. A gold pin, a swan with a long, sinuous neck, a diamond for an eye, a delicate, old-fashioned trinket that must, I suddenly realize, have belonged to her mother.

I mention the pin.

"Yes, my mother's," she says, reading my thoughts. "I've come here today to talk about her. I don't think I have been honest, before now, giving you the impression I didn't remember her. I think I remembered her but didn't want to."

She begins to talk in a voice one could (almost) call animated; twenty minutes pass, she is still talking. I have never heard her say so much at any one time before. After a half hour, she seems breathless, but eager to continue. Ten minutes before the session is up, she looks exhausted. Her pale, remote, expressionless face has acquired the faintest darkness beneath the eyes, as if, throughout this storytelling, she has been living in herself. She glances at the clock with a look of astonishment. "Time to go? Time to go? But I haven't even begun yet. . . ."

She remembers her mother standing at the window, holding a

lace curtain in her left hand, gazing out into the garden. The image is not clear, the light coming through the window seems to pass through her mother, making her luminous and transparent. The little girl on the bed is worried that when the light fades her mother will vanish. She feels this in her throat, it is like something that has got caught there and is scratching to get out.

"Fear," I say.

"Fear," she repeats. "Yes. Yes. I was afraid."

She makes an extra appointment, comes early the next day, is waiting for me in the garden. She begins to talk before we get into the room. "My father should have spoken about her. That would have helped me to know I remembered. It is important for a girl to remember her mother. Without a mother, one feels one has never been born oneself. Maybe she was strange, a strange person, or perhaps crazy, but that doesn't matter. That's what the neighbor used to say. She told me that. I'm sure she told me that. But it doesn't matter. She was my mother and I deserved to have her."

She stands next to her chair and so I stand next to mine. It is a day on which conventions will be broken. "My mother would like it here," she says, "maybe one day I will be able to bring her."

"But you have brought her. So vividly. The woman standing at the window, the little girl afraid to lose her. . . ."

"Ah yes," she says, confidingly, "but that is not the same."

"No," I agree. "It would be better if we could have her here with us."

"Then you agree? I should bring her?"

It is my turn to be confused. The question seems so insistent, driving at something concrete, tangible. I have been speaking in metaphor. Sylvia, it occurs to me, never does.

"Bring her? How do you mean, bring her?"

71

"I've decided to go to the hospital and get her out."

I hold on to my chair. The atmosphere in the room is so charged I think the sheer force of what I do not understand will knock me over. I am frightened that this infinitely lonely woman has finally broken, that the memory I took for progress, the beginning of storytelling, the recollection of childhood, has pushed her over the edge.

"Sylvia," I say, "why don't we sit down."

"But you will let me bring her?"

"I thought we were talking about your mother? I thought she was dead."

"Oh, no, not dead. Taken away. Taken away. And I remember. The whole thing, the day it happened. That's what I've come to tell you about."

She sits down carefully in her chair, smooths her skirt over her knees, talks softly.

"My mother, that day, had been walking up and down the stairs. Up and down the stairs. I don't know if she'd done it before. Maybe that was something she did often. I remember her standing at the window, and I remember her, on that day, the last day I ever saw her, walking up and down the stairs. I stood at the door to my room. I watched her. She kept wringing her hands. Sometimes, she would put her hands to her cheeks and make the strangest sound. Once or twice I came out of my room and stood on the stairs so that she would have to see me. She walked past. I have the impression she walked right through me, as if I had never come into existence for her, but I know that is not possible. She just walked past, as if I weren't there. When my father came home she was in her room, with the door locked. We could hear that she was breaking and smashing things. She kept making that strange sound. My father knocked at the door but she wouldn't open. When they finally came to get her, they came in by a ladder, they broke the window to her room. I ran downstairs into the garden to see what was happening. They brought my mother down by the ladder. Her wrists and legs were tied. She had gone limp, she didn't struggle. She kept making that strange sound. I don't think I've ever heard that sound again since. But I think, if now I were to give it a name, I would say my mother was . . . moaning."

The silence that follows this story does not fill up with emptiness or desolation. Sylvia sits very still but she is looking at me. Her eyes, which have often seemed so distant and impenetrable, now look gentle and sad.

"The poor woman," she says.

"And the poor little girl."

"That's true," she agrees. "I feel sorry for them both."

A few weeks later she says, "I've decided the time has come. I don't care what the trustees say. I am her daughter, her only living relative. And I will take care of her."

Her mother had been living in an expensive, private mental hospital, on the Peninsula. She had been there for thirty years. She did not recognize her daughter when she arrived to visit. Sylvia expected this. We had gone over it, rehearsing it, practicing for it, anticipating it. Sylvia was impressed by how much she and her mother resembled one another.

"We look alike. That's what matters. What matters for now is that I know she is my mother. I was always afraid to visit her before. I never let myself think about her. My father made it clear we should never mention her and so I never did. Even after he died I didn't let myself think about her. I probably didn't want to think about the day she was taken away. . . ."

Thirty years. Her mother had been in the mental hospital for over thirty years. During that time, she had not been visited by any member of her family. Later, it turned out that the neighbor, whose husband had left her, who used to stay with Sylvia when she was small, occasionally came to visit. The mother was supported by a trust, which should, by all accounts, have had a great deal of money left in it. The fact that very little money was left made it easier for Sylvia to secure her mother's release. Using the considerable skills she had acquired as an executive secretary, she contacted several lawyers and eventually decided not to challenge the trustees about the financial status of the trust if they would agree to have her mother discharged from the hospital into her care. She hired a nurse to care for her mother while she was at work, moved into a new, larger apartment on the ground floor, asked for and got a raise and one day told me that she would never again wonder why people went on living. She described in meticulous detail the French doors that opened into a well-tended garden. "I did not want my mother to live in a house with stairs. I didn't want her to stand looking out the window. Now, whenever she wants to go outside, she goes out. I've given the nurse precise instructions. It is our job to bring my mother back to life. Then, I will teach her how to be my mother."

A few weeks after she had brought her mother home she first came up with the phrase, "I have given birth to my mother." She, however, denies this.

She came in later for our session, flustered, unsettled, but sure of her ground. "I know, I shouldn't be late. But this was important. I thought surely you would understand."

"You haven't ever been even one minute late in the two some years we've been speaking together."

She smiled faintly and came as close, perhaps, as this woman will ever come to a roguish expression. "Perhaps I have never had a reason to be late before."

"Oh, I can't wait to hear. What was it?"

"I've given birth to my mother."

"You've given birth to your mother? Oh, I see what you mean. You brought her out of the hospital, you've brought her out of a living death, you've brought her back to life. . . ."

"Maybe." She considers this judiciously. "But what I mean is, I'm teaching her, for the first time, how to be a mother. That's what she could never figure out before. And that's what made her so troubled."

Sylvia remembers this conversation differently. In her version, when I ask her what has made her late, she replies, "I've been helping my mother to become a mother."

I say: "Oh? You've given birth to your mother?"

She says: "My mother never knew how to take care of a little child. She was a little child herself. That's how my father always treated her. So how could she suddenly know how to take care of me?"

Sometimes it takes two people to have an idea. In that sense, it does not matter to whom the idea belongs; if it occurred for the first time in conversation between them, both will have to assume responsibility for it.

Sylvia's story does not match up precisely with the grand scheme of the mother-story I have sketched out earlier. For her, nothing came station by station through repetitive sequences that led to a new birth of the self. Instead, it all came in a rush: memory, stories, fragments of stories, details hard to place in context. Chance played a part in it too. I ran into her by chance in a café; this spontaneous recognition reawakened a crucial sensitivity from her childhood. She began to remember. Then she immediately acted. This woman, who had seemed so remote from life, so incapable of spontaneous action or self-declaration, went into motion with a zealousness that made me think she had finally discovered her long-absent life's purpose. She went to visit her mother; she went to visit this woman whom she had spoken about as if she were dead without ever literally telling me that she had died. She was a mother for whom her daughter had never been born. The daughter, in turn, had never existed for herself. To have a life, to come to life, to enter into her own sensations and feelings, she would first have to persuade her mother that she, the daughter, was alive. That is how we saw it much later, when together, toward the end of our work, we were thinking back on all that had occurred.

As Sylvia brings her mother back to life, she also painstakingly pieces together the infinitely lonely passages of her childhood. She was never shut up in a room by herself, never locked in without language or stimulation, but that is how, as a child, her life often felt to her. Now that she has begun to attach language to her experience, she can describe with astonishing precision experiences that had been excluded from language until now. As a listener, it impresses me that as she brings into words the desolation and emptiness that were her earliest environment, the suffocating impression of them, which she earlier needed me to experience, is gone. She describes, and feels, but I no longer do, the endless awful drift of dust motes through a light beam in a room from which all the life has been sucked away. Her mother is there, but absent; she is, in every memory, transparent, never present in the flesh, "hollow" and "without a touchable surface." If the child, who has learned to be absolutely still, without needs, expressions, gestures, movements, should ever try to move toward her, engage her, or touch her, the mother "becomes a slippery surface, from which all contact rolls off." To sit in a room with her is to experience nonpresence that becomes indistinguishable from nonexistence. There is no time, nothing moves, nothing passes, the dust motes in the light beam freeze in an endless static emptiness from which there is no retreat.

The child, grown up now, says, "My connection with my mother was through absence. Because I learned to be absent too I had in some sense joined her. My mother and I lived a living death together. There are many ways to think about this now. Perhaps, it would be fair to say, neither of us had ever been born. When my mother began to break down, when she started walking up and down the stairs, that restlessness was the first sign of her coming back to life. But then we shut her away and it is up to me now to bring her back."

"You say 'we' shut her away?"

"If I am completely honest, I have to admit that I was relieved. I was free of her. I was set free. I went to school. I could breathe. Before that, sitting in the room with her, I remember how hard I tried to stifle my breath, to stop my heart beating. Stillness, perfect, unchanging stillness was what she seemed to require. So yes, I have to say, indeed, yes, I was relieved when she was taken away."

Sylvia tells me that she does not wish for any other life than taking care of her mother. People have always found her strange, she herself has never felt a connection to them. Friendship, dating, parties, marriage, children seem to her "beyond my reach." She hopes that I will not be disappointed if our work does not succeed in making these possible for her. She imagines I think she is motivated by guilt, from which it would be better if she could free herself. She hopes I will let her go on the way she is going. "Even guilt," she says to me one day as she is leaving the room, "gives a reason to go on living. Guilt is a feeling. You have to do something about it. Imagine that I spend the rest of my life trying to make things up to my mother because I neglected her all those years. Is that so terrible?"

Sylvia has learned how to smile. It is a subtle expression, which you might miss if you did not know her well. It pinches slightly the corners of her mouth, giving them the very faintest ironic curl. "Has anyone ever figured out how to distinguish guilt from love?" she asks, turning back as I stand watching her at the door. Then she goes on without waiting for a response, out the gate, which she shuts carefully behind her.

In the way Sylvia cares for her mother I can tell that she is doing for the older woman exactly what she might have wished the mother had done for her as a child. She has taken over all the practical care of her mother, even coming home for lunch to sit with her while she eats. In the beginning, her mother has to be fed and Sylvia wants this feeding to come from her. She bathes, dresses, combs, tends her mother, although the advice from doctors at the hospital has been clear on this point. She should encourage her mother to do as much as she can for herself. Sylvia does not agree. "First things first," Sylvia pronounces. Mother is now going to have the childhood Sylvia missed. Sylvia, through her mother, will reverse the severe neglect of her own childhood. "Mother is taking care of me by letting me take care of her. That is our beginning. We'll see how far we can go."

Evenings and weekends Sylvia sits with her mother without

speaking. Her mother has not spoken for thirty years. Sylvia has taught herself to knit so that she can keep busy in her mother's presence. She plays music, she sings along, every so often she sits still and "gazes" at the older woman, who seems remarkably un-aged, as if she had shut herself away from time and had not lived through the thirty silent years. Always slender, pale, still, large-eyed and absent, she does not seem strange to Sylvia, who pa-tiently waits for a sign that her mother has noticed her.

I suggest Sylvia contact a support group for people who are caring for aging parents. Perhaps they will have some suggestions that might be helpful. Sylvia says, "I guess you believe in reincar-nation. You seem to be thinking of the life I will lead when I come back after this one."

Her sense of what is possible for her is consistently opposed to my occasional efforts to expand the scope of her social life. Even-tually, I settle down and enter the slow, painstaking process with her. This is the life she has chosen. It is the first meaningful life she has ever known. She has no doubt about seeing it through. On the day she arrives to tell me that her mother deliberately reached out to touch her hand, it is clear that her sense of accomplishment, her pleasure, her pride, her muted happiness, surpass anything she has ever experienced before. It is, she believes, the first deliber-ate acknowledgment of her existence she has ever received from her mother. If Sylvia is right, this light, almost impalpable touch, has brought into being, for the first time in their history, a mother and daughter.

In this story, it would be hard to say who has given birth to whom.

8

.

other-stories tend to have a dominant thematic, a heart-core around which the story is spun. You never know what you will find when you start to listen. Will it be a tale in which an anguished guilt predominates? An unappeasable longing for an absent, vanished, unattainable mother? As a listener, you may enter an underground of shifting, paradoxical, uncertain growth. The story seems overgrown, in need of pruning. But what should be cut? Every word might be a key, a code, a narrow passage to something indispensable.

I heard this next story, Helene's story, many years ago. I wasn't a serious collector back then, I didn't have a book in mind. Recently, when I sat down to take notes, I found this voice, with the wild, obsessive, torrential quality of the speaker. She had been introduced to me by the friend of a friend, with the warning to be careful, once I got her started it would be hard to get her to stop. Getting her to stop was the last thing I had in mind. My memory has held on to her with a rich store of details, recording (I hope accurately) her strange speech rhythms, the wonderful repetitions that carry a sometimes shocking emotional intensity, as the story drives home to its ever-elusive, confessional goal. Sometimes, rushing to keep up with the urgency of the voice, I have asked myself whether the story fits into my pattern. What is the precise moment when this daughter gives birth to a symbolic mother? Is it now? Is it later? Does it happen? Does it matter? Maybe the story itself is the birth, or the act of telling it so desperately to a perfect stranger.

WHAT HELENE SAID

You want me to talk about my mother? You sure that's what you want? If you knew me well, you would have heard this story half a dozen times. I have a friend, who is no longer actually my friend, who is not my friend because she was sick to death of how much I talked about my mother. When I heard about you, collecting stories, I thought, Here's my chance, someone who actually wants to listen. I still can't believe it. I'm still waiting for that certain look in your eyes. That look. It means time to stop but once I get going I can't stop myself. I think I'm going to say something new, I start out with a new idea, maybe even an insight, but before long I'm back into the old obsession.

My mother was, and maybe she still is, the most beautiful woman in the world. We always said she looked like Lena Horne, but I think she was even more beautiful. When I was little I liked to sit in her room when she was talking on the telephone and stare at her. I had two younger sisters, tomboys, who were never interested in the same things that interested my mother and me. We were always looking in fashion magazines, cutting out pictures. I had a whole scrapbook made up of bits and pieces of pictures of women. This one with the perfect hair, this one with gorgeous lips and so on. I didn't know the word for it at the time but I was making collages and the idea was to produce the perfect woman. My mother got a big kick out of this because somehow, no matter how much I cut and pasted, the women all tended to come out looking like her.

There was another curious feature. I wasn't concerned with racial characteristics, I would pick out any kind of lips or nose or hair that appealed to me and paste it together with another part of a woman's face. My sisters thought I was really an idiot. They were out playing games, or ball, or running around and I was sitting on the floor in my mother's bedroom, on this beautiful plush carpet, leaning against her knees, thumbing through magazines. I don't think my mother ever actually joined in, but I always thought about it as a shared project.

Later on, when you think back about those things, you can have a lot of different interpretations. When I went to college, in the sixties, and I told my new friends about the scrapbook, one of them thought I was trying to put together the perfect upper-middle-class white woman as a model for myself, but I don't think so. I think I wanted to blend all the races into a single perfect strain, which I could then imagine my mother and I belonged to. When people said I looked just like her I would go a little crazy inside. I don't know what it means to this day, but practically nothing has ever interested me as much as that scrapbook. I guess if I had become an artist, and went on to paint or sculpt, it might make some kind of sense, as if I had been preparing myself. Instead, I became a dancer and then a stage designer and that's what I am now. So what did it all mean? It's still a question. My mother and I definitely obsessed with female beauty, and she was the most beautiful woman either one of us had ever seen, and I could tell she thought that from the way she studied herself in the mirror, I've never, ever, seen another woman look at herself like that. Not as if she was in love with herself. The look was cool, appraising, but gratified. She studied herself with an enormous detachment, objectively, critically, but with satisfaction. It was impossible to get her attention. My sisters could race into the room, wrestle, jump on the bed, none of which was allowed, and which they did just to provoke her, which was impossible, so I guess it had become a game of some kind, to see whether it was possible to disrupt her, and it was not. It was not possible. That's our family story. It might be exaggerated but maybe not, maybe not.

Here's the place I like to get stuck, which drives my friends crazy. I've done you the great favor of just saying my mother looked like Lena Horne, but my usual way is to try to describe her, I get all caught up in it, to this day, because I have this image before my eyes, I literally still dream about my mother. . . . Go ahead? Describe her? You sure you know what you're asking for? Well, you don't ever have to see me again anyway so what difference does it make if I drive you away? The problem is that I can't, no matter how hard I try, even if I am looking straight at a picture of her, I can't describe what I see, because it isn't only on the surface, although it is of course also on the surface, some way the individual features, beautiful in themselves, discover an almost . . . an almost shocking harmony together. The way my mother is beautiful always reminds you of something else. You can't really look at her because you are immediately trying to figure out what it is she reminds you of. I don't mean Lena Horne, who really has the same kind of beauty, similar in evoking something you feel you've been wanting to see all your life and there, suddenly, you look at this woman and there it is. What's strange is that you could have this experience with my mother living in the same house with her and seeing her every day. I know my father felt that way. He and I used to stand at the bottom of the stairs when she was going out just to watch her come downstairs and I can tell you we were having the same experience, as if my mother were almost a stranger, transformed by a new pair of earrings, or a new gown or the way she carried her head, you could almost think she was not the mother you had grown up with, but something exotic, always she would invoke something from far, far away and I know this was also how my father felt, although he never said so. We would hold hands, he and I, and I am sure we were too well behaved to let our mouths fall open, but that is how I tend to remember us, proud, we were very, very proud of her, as if we had our own household goddess.

We were very well off when I was growing up, my mother still is, although my father is dead and she is remarried, to another man who is a black professional. My father was one of the first black men to go to medical school, he was remarkably good at what he did and he even had white patients, he did, hard to believe as it is, because that was in the fifties. We had two maids, who lived with us, in a wing of the house, which they had to themselves. One of them was there to do the ironing. That's all she did. She ironed our sheets, tablecloths, handkerchiefs, my father's shirts; every one of us, even my sisters who could have cared less, wore perfectly ironed underclothes. My mother never slept in the same sheets twice . . . well, that's an exaggeration or rather the opposite, an under-ation. She rarely made it through the night in the same pair of sheets. We were our own private laundry. Patricia, the maid, was the busiest person in our house, although the other woman had to manage everything else, except the cook of course or the chauffeur. If you ask what all this busyness was for, you'd have to say, I looking back would have to say, it supported one woman's remarkable beauty. Because my father was a doctor, my mother got involved with plastic surgery before there was any fashion for it. She believed in it unquestioningly, as if it were her purpose here on earth to preserve, protect and cultivate her beauty and I'm not so sure she was wrong. If you were in a room with my mother you felt . . . it's hard to describe . . . I could say . . . she was the reason for being there, no matter what else important or significant was taking place, or whoever else was present, the reason to be there, what really mattered and meant something was my mother.

What kind of effect did this have on me? I told you that as I started to grow up people started to say I looked like her, which was true in a way, if you went feature by feature, only something was missing in me that was there in my mother. . . . I always knew I could never aspire to her level and that was the only accomplishment I wanted to have. Why did I want to have it? I think I wanted my mother to be as fascinated with me as I was with her. My sisters went their own way, one of them is an engineer, the other teaches comparative literature at Colgate University, and then there's me, a wanna-be dancer, but what have I ever really accomplished? I have lived my life, that's what I could say now, my whole life, in some sense, that's what I think, standing at the foot of the stairs gazing at my mother, proud that she's mine and at the same time, at the very same moment, knowing that I will never accomplish anything as extraordinary as she did. I've tried to be a feminist; I believe women get a raw, rough deal in our society, but I can't shake off the idea that beauty is not only a patriarchal standard or requirement for women, there's something godlike about it, a divine gift, beautiful people, and especially beautiful women, have been given one of the rarest gifts in the world, which we others are meant to worship and appreciate, which we do, although we know in our feminist heart of hearts that we shouldn't. So, the effect on me was I'm still there, at the foot of the stairs, although I've had back then some success of my own and it was because of beauty, or what passes for beauty if you didn't know my mother. Okay, I'll stop there. No need to lose a friend before I make one.

An example . . . an example. . . . I am fourteen, just past the awkward age, teeth straight as a row of tombstones, hair growing long, long legs, my very own long legs. What happens? Suddenly, I'm my mother's new preoccupation. My mother is obsessively interested in me. Of course it's easy to say, when you grow up and you get sophisticated, well sure, I'm an extension of my mother, but that's not how it felt. It felt fantastic. It felt like I had finally succeeded in getting my mother's gaze out of that mirror and onto me. Getting me dressed, picking out my clothes, deciding on my hairstyle. Suddenly, I am important as she is. Maybe more important. She decides she will hire a personal maid, whom we will share, although the maid was mainly intended for me. Her beauty had already been perfected, mine needed work. To cultivate beauty is a high art, my mother respected me because I knew how to respect my looks, but she couldn't know, because I would never, never have told her, that I felt uncomfortable in my own skin, as if I didn't belong there. My good looks seemed borrowed, not an intrinsic part of me the way hers were, mine seemed laid-on, mine were a pale reflection of a sun-goddess mother, I couldn't figure out if I was proud to look like her or ashamed that since I looked like her she set the standard I would be measured by and I could never approach. My sisters just took off. After my father died we almost never heard from them. It was just my mother and me, the maids, the big house, we still gave dinner parties, at which I was the center of attention to the degree that my being grown up, and my mother looking like my sister, that now became the center of conversation, so I was involved too, although of course the real point was my mother. Of course, we knew all the famous black actors and writers and businessmen and doctors and lawyers, not that there are so many, but more than you'd think, so it was really something to see two women, without doing anything other than just being there, holding up their end of the conversation because my mother was a very well-educated woman and she was intelligent, that was part of her charm, it still is, to hear these very intelligent comments coming out of such a beautiful mouth.

Where am I? Where am I? You see what I mean? I was going to tell you about the time when I was fourteen years old. We moved into a very exclusive white part of town. We were the first black people in the neighborhood, we said Negro then; the neighborhood, which was segregated, maybe unofficially, but still we were the first and I was the first Negro girl ever to go to that high school. My mother took me to a counselor the whole summer before school began so we could prepare for the reception I was likely to get. That would have been . . . nineteen fifty . . . two! We were way ahead of the civil rights movement and we didn't think of ourselves as some kind of pioneers. My mother wanted to live in that neighborhood, my father bought a beautiful house, and we moved. And I had to go to school. I suppose I could have gone to private school, but maybe everyone wanted to see what it would be like to send a girl like me into a school like that and I was ready for it. My sisters insisted on going to their old school, the chauffeur drove them back to our old neighborhood, which was not exactly an impoverished part of town, as you can imagine, but I went to the new high school.

I don't have to tell you how my mother and I prepared. We spent the summer with the counselor and studying French and shopping. I think my mother wanted everyone to imagine I had some kind of French background, so because of that, and wanting to please her, my French got very good. We used to speak to each other in French in front of the maids. And when we were shopping. Every time we saw something that caught my mother's attention, she'd buy it and have it sent home for me to wear "for the first day at school." I had enough clothes for "the first day at school" to last through college, not that she would have sent me off without a new wardrobe, if I had been willing to go. I wouldn't go until my sisters had already graduated, and they were my younger sisters. Then I went for one year and quit. We are approaching the pathetic part of this story. But let's stick with fourteen years old.

I'm not going to go into that first day at school. I don't want to go into that again. If you want to hear about it you can ask my ex-friends. The chauffeur, of course, dropped me off and you can be sure that our car, which was always polished to a high shine, was rubbed up so high . . . Everyone had heard by then that this new girl was coming to school and she was a NE-gro, and they were looking, you can just imagine, how they were looking and I, I don't know how I managed it, I must have just pretended I was my mother coming down those stairs, I got out of that car, I took my books from the chauffeur, who knew, believe me, that was one sharp man, what an exceptional role he'd been called on to play, and I walked into that school. Through the front door, into the principal's office, as my mother had arranged, and he came with me to my first class, to introduce me.

In those days, I don't know what it's like now, but back then we had social clubs in high school and they were arranged in a very strict hierarchy and not many girls got invited to pledge for the

89

best of them or even for any of them, most of the girls in that school were definitely excluded, or didn't want to join, which was probably true for some of them. I know my sisters, if they had been at that school, wouldn't have cared less. I cared, my mother cared, we knew I would never get into those clubs, but what happened? I was actually rushed for every one of the snobby society clubs, which is what my mother had secretly hoped and secretly predicted. Not that she'd tell my father a thing like that. He wouldn't have wanted her to use me in that way. But I never objected. It was our victory, my mother's and mine. When I came home with the club's pin, the club my mother and I decided was the only club worth joining, we put it on the table between us, we said nothing, we just looked at one another, and looked at the pin and burst out laughing. We didn't have to say anything. What for? If you have to spell out a triumph, it is not much of a triumph.

I know it is not simply a question of beauty, but I still think, to this day, how would it have gone if I hadn't been what my mother made me?

You might think this story is leading up to something tragic. It is only leading up to something pathetic and this is the part I haven't told anyone before, so I guess my friend was right in suggesting I talk to you. Pathetic, because I could just not leave home. I am the one that got stuck, who stayed behind, tied to my mother's apron strings as they used to say, not that she ever wore an apron. I am the one who could never leave her, especially not after my father died. She would have sent me to the best colleges in the world, I had good grades, I spoke French, I could have gone anywhere, but I went to the local state college because I didn't want to go away from home because I already knew nothing in life was going to be as interesting to me as my mother, I didn't want to leave her, it wasn't hidden, nothing you have to dig out after years of analysis, I just didn't want to go away from her. I used to count the hours I was away in school, thinking, three more, two more, one more and I'm out of here, I'm on the way home. My mother was always waiting, we'd go out for lunch or tea or shopping and of course everyone thought they had never seen such a close mother and daughter, except that, as I see it now, were we ever a mother and daughter and not just a mother and her reflection?

What do I mean? Do I know what I mean? I say these things, I don't have to understand them. One day it all fell apart and I am the one who is responsible for it because I introduced my mother to him, I met him first, we were at a party, dressed alike, in different shades of the same Dior dress, because we liked to make that kind of a sensation and I was, I don't know, I was probably by then twenty-eight years old, still living at home, still living off my mother although that is not how she thought of it or I thought of it, we just went on as we had always done, living together and then I met him first and I introduced them. I had the oddest feeling, I watched them talking, I excused myself to get a drink so I could look at them and I knew, absolutely knew, for certain, that man was going to change my life and he did. That's what happened. Because after that, I suppose you could see this coming, my mother dropped me. She didn't have time for me. She was in love, in some way she'd never been in love with my father, this man was a younger man, she was getting older and she needed him, the way she might earlier have needed me, to reflect back something about herself she liked to see in another person. Suddenly, I hated her. Everything changed. I thought I had been used and exploited my whole life. I was still living at home, in the same bedroom I had since high school, I had never worked, I had no idea how to go out into the world, and that is what I mean by pathetic. I just hung on there while she went off into a new life, his world, his attention and no one had any time for me and why should they? I could see so clearly that my mother had never loved me, she never loved anyone until she met this man, she had used me, not even as an extension of herself, which implies some distance, some separation between us, whereas I was nothing but her reflection, she looked at me to see herself, to perfect herself in me and when she didn't need me anymore she dropped me.

Finally, I moved out and I moved in with a woman I had met in college, who had sort of kept in touch with me. I'd like to say I cut myself off from my mother but of course I did not. She still gave me my allowance and I still . . . I waited at home . . . I didn't go out or make dates or friends all that much or anything because I was still waiting for my mother's attention, for her to call, which she'd do whenever he was out of town on business and I'd go over, tail between my legs, because I still hadn't found anything that was as interesting to me as my mother. I just missed her. I left her house and I pined for her, that's the pathetic part. And it gets worse. I had done some dancing by then, so I could justify the way I was living by thinking that I was an artist and was devoted to my art, but I don't think I was ever as devoted to anything I did when I was grown up, as I had been devoted to that scrapbook. I would sit at home, drinking diet Cokes, waiting for the phone to ring. Pathetic. Because of course sooner or later it would, she would need me, she'd want company, she felt lonely, she missed the good old days, we'd fly back together and I was always happy. I just didn't want those times to end. That was my life.

This woman I shared a flat with began to talk to me. She pointed out how I was not living, so that I could always be available to my mother. She thought I should get help and because I wouldn't I guess she tried to help me. She was the first friend I lost over my mother. After that, there was a boyfriend but how could he, a mere man, compete with my mother? And then I fell in love with a woman, if you could call love what I was capable of in those days, and it was she who really opened my eyes. Because I still went running whenever my mother called. I'd drop whatever we were doing, or planning to do, and little by little my lover made me aware that it was a choice between her and my mother, I couldn't just pick her up and drop her again every time my mother beckoned and I almost came apart over that. My lover left me, and I just couldn't stand it. I'd grown attached to her, something that could never happen before. I tried to win her back. I swore I'd break with my mother, who had gotten used to using me, especially now that she was getting older, and was definitely trying to hold on. She offered to buy me a house, she actually bought me a very expensive car for my birthday, which my lover, when we were together again, wanted me to give back and I just couldn't. But we survived that and then my mother invited us to go to Europe. Her husband was going to be away on a business trip and my mother had this great idea that the three of us, she and my lover and me, would go to Europe together. My lover said no, but my mother got really charming, she booked us into the best hotels in the world, started taking us out shopping, started charming my lover and now my lover started to see how my mother was really irresistible when she half made up her mind to be, but before this she hadn't been interested in my lover but now she was. So we're going, we have tickets, we're going to fly to New York and stay in the X hotel and take a Concorde jet to Paris and my lover just won't go. Suddenly, she sees what's happening to us, we're being bought, we're being used, my mother is coming between us and maybe my lover thought she was falling in love with my mother, which can happen, believe me, and she just refused to go.

So there's my choice. Totally pathetic. I'm almost forty years old and I am going to have to choose between my lover and my mother!

What do I do? I don't know how or why exactly I did it, or how I became capable of it, but I chose my lover. I called my mother and told her that we weren't going to Europe with her. I apologized, I tried to explain how it was for Kyle and me and my mother went out of her mind! I'd never seen her like that. It's possible, in our whole life together, I'd never opposed her before. She hung up on me and told me she never wanted to see me again. I thought she meant it. I went running over there, she didn't want to let me in but of course it had been my house for so long I knew how to get in without even needing a key, and I probably still had the key on me, why wouldn't I? So we had our reconciliation, and I tried to get her to go on with me even if we didn't go to Europe and there was no way I could get her to hold on to the bond. She was ready to break with me over something like that. But I couldn't give in. Somehow things had just gone too far, it seemed too preposterous, having to buy a relationship with your own mother. I went back to my own house and the phone started to ring and I didn't answer. It was the first time in my life I didn't answer my mother's call. I sat up all night, shaking. My lover stayed up with me. It was as if I was trying to withdraw from something, giving up a fixation, a drug, an attachment, and it was just shaking me apart.

So this is the night I wanted to tell you about. This is the point of all this talking. This is what I have been trying to get to. I guess I would have had a few more friends if I had gotten here sooner. That night was like passing through a nightmare tunnel. If you survived it, if you got to the other side, you would come out into your own life and then the shadow of that other life, the way I had always lived in my mother's shadow, all that would be over. But did I want it to be over?

Kyle, my lover, didn't close her eyes the whole night, she was right there, literally holding on to me, which you had to do if I was going to get through because I kept on shaking with this kind of shaking you don't see every day, from the finest little tremors to the whole body heaving and jumping, I'm not exaggerating, you can ask Kyle. Well, she kept talking to me. I couldn't tell you what all she said, the more I shake, the more she talks and finally I can feel I'm coming out of it, just this smallest, tiniest, teeniest something different inside of the shaking like my cells, or the cells of my cells know I am going to make it, there's another side to it, I'll get through, I'll come out over there, wherever there is if you know what I mean.

Okay, you get it. You get it. What Kyle said? She's said it since, believe me. About me being the sacrifice to my mother, me going through the stuff my mother couldn't feel and I could see somehow that Kyle was right, what I was feeling, this incredible, this indescribable terror of losing my mother, breaking the bond, shattering everything between us, is what my mother must have always felt, it was my mother who had always been clinging to me, not the other way around, I had been protecting her from her fear of being abandoned, it sounds funny when you try to repeat it. I had been taking up all the feelings she couldn't have or didn't want to have, so she left them to me, they had become my feelings

95

and I was now, for the first time, shaking them loose, even though I thought I would probably lose her and I did, I did, I'm here to tell you, I did.

So, I came out on the other side, yes I did, but my mother and I, we didn't. Of course, no mother is actually going to break with her daughter over not taking a trip to Europe. What would she say to her friends? But from that time until this day, and it is now a good four years later, my mother and I have never again had one of our marvelous times together. We do the same things but there is always a distance, a reserve, a coldness, as if we had broken apart and become two separate people who are not going to be able to fall back into the illusion that they are one blissful harmonious soul, united forever, twin beauties, only one of them is just enough less beautiful to make the other, older woman, shine ever brighter in her loveliness. I never did manage to tell you how my mother looks, did I? but okay, okay, I won't try again, because this is the point at which I drive people crazy, and you would think, you really would, that I'd be over that by now, wanting to capture this image I have in my mind which is indescribable. The most beautiful woman in the world, what else is there to say? For me, the hard part is always being tempted, to this day I'm still tempted to patch things up with her, do anything she wants, come and go the way I used to whenever she beckons, in the hope that one of those smiles would light on me again, or that caressing gesture, or the way she suddenly would fling her arm around my shoulder and put her head over next to mine, no one else is ever going to make me feel like that, not even Kyle, it's just not possible because Kyle and I, we know, we are two separate people, eternally divided from an eternal harmony which my mother and I, well, when we had it, we had it, absolute perfection, believe it or not, that's up to you, but I tell you, whenever I think about it, I don't know how I keep myself from just running back over and crawling and fawning and doing whatever I have to do to get her back.

The sad part, the pathetic part, the part that shouldn't have worked out that way, is how I, to the degree I understand her, and now I do, I understand what is inside her, I can't help but forgive her and that is what tempts me the most, to run back to forgive her for this dreadful waste of my whole life, which is not yet over, although my life is for sure half over, because I'm still only on my way to whatever I might find, and meanwhile what I have to go through is still fighting off the incredible pull of my mother, because now I know, because I have felt it myself, how bad, deep inside, this beautiful woman was always feeling.

This is my mother! I'm talking about my mother! But that's how I feel and now it's out, I've told you, you've heard it and the good thing I can say about myself is, I, feeling like that, I, feeling the way I just told you, I don't go back fawning and crawling, I let it be, I go my own way, such as that is, trying to make a life for myself, SUCH AS IT IS. . . .

CHAPTER 9

JUANA'S STORY

The First Session

She has come to see me because she is having trouble finishing a novel. She has told me this over the telephone and repeats it as we sit down at my desk. She bends over to take the manuscript out of a bag, holds it with clenched fists above the desk for a moment before setting it down with an audible *thwock*. "So there," she says. "We've made it. What do I do now?"

"Up to you. You can read to me, or you can tell me about it or about where you've run into trouble."

"Up to me? If it were up to me the whole thing would be on its way to the dump. . . ." She crooks a thumb at the wastebasket. "To the dump. To the dump. Not that I mean it. If I meant it I wouldn't be here, would I?"

"Probably not. But that wastebasket has been full to overflowing before now with a lot of stuff that saw its way to the dump before it saw its way out into the world."

"I knew you'd get it. Okay, I'll read."

She reads with a rough, bitter edge to her voice; the manuscript and what it contains has become, it seems, her dearest enemy. She turns the pages with a contemptuous flip of her index finger. Once in a while she interrupts her reading to address the manuscript directly. "You shouldn't be in here. What are you doing there? I thought I had taken you out."

I am witnessing a lover's quarrel. The manuscript, mute, unprotesting, receives her reproaches passively. It is a long-suffering, silent partner to a painful relationship that has got stuck. I myself feel some affection for the manuscript, which just now is being scratched at with a pen the writer has picked up from my desk. "Wait a minute. Wait a minute," the writer says to the page. "That's not how it goes. Hold on there, let's get this right."

She is a tough, large woman with a bushy head of curly hair, she probably works out, has wonderfully developed muscular arms which are, I imagine, intimidating to the manuscript. Feeling protective toward it, I gather up a few pages and read them back to her.

"Whoa there," she says, "what are you up to? It sounds really weird coming out in someone else's voice."

"I have the impression you've never read this. Never really paid attention to it as itself. You remind me of one of those mothers who is constantly adjusting the kid's hair, wiping her nose, pulling up or down at her socks. . . ."

"Hey, you got it. Okay, let's listen."

She leans way back in her chair, narrows her eyes and fixes her gaze on me. "Stop there, stop there," she blurts out after a page or two. "How can anyone listen to this stuff?"

"You maybe are having trouble listening. But I'm not."

"Okay, what are you trying to tell me?" She gives the manuscript on the desk a hard poke.

There is something contagious about her boisterous manner. "Leave the poor thing alone," I say, patting it gently. "The problem is not in here."

"Ha ha!" she cries out, leaning toward me, tapping on her head. "In here, you mean? Oh sister, are you ever tactful. Okay, that's what I'm here for. Deliver the diagnosis."

"You have a voice. The story is compelling. You keep interrupting it but I'd like to hear how it goes on."

"You'd like to hear how it goes on. . . . You really mean it?"

"Why not? I was getting engaged. A woman, who has never seen her birth mother, is writing her a letter. She's introducing herself. She has no idea whether the woman will want to see her. What if she doesn't remember? What if she . . ."

Something has just happened in the room. The impression is so strong I turn my head to see if someone has entered through the window or the door into the garden. The room looks back blandly, unaware of intrusion. When I turn back to meet her gaze, I am startled by the change in her appearance. She's a big, florid woman with a head of energetically curling hair, who now gives the impression that she has removed an ill-fitting coat, shrugged it off while my head was turned, as if it were a purely protective, outer aspect of her personality. An expression I would not have expected has appeared on her face. It is . . . suspicion perhaps? Something guarded, aware of danger, checking things out? She seems less robust and somehow smaller, as if she had visibly changed size and takes up less space in her chair.

"Do you really want to know why I am here?" she asks, in a voice conspicuously subdued.

"I want to know, definitely. What's up?"

"I chose you," she says, "very carefully. Not only so you could help me with the novel."

"What was it about me?"

"Seven particular things," she says, raising her hands to count

101

them off. "You come from a background without money, like mine. That's important."

"That's true, there wasn't money in my family."

"I know. I read your books. Your parents were immigrants. That's important. My father was what used to be called a wet-back, he came in here illegally from Mexico, married an American woman, had American children. He was entitled to citizenship but there were problems because of his left-wing activities. You see what I'm driving at? We came from the same family background. You're about my age. You have had training as a psychoanalyst. That matters, boy that matters. I have a question to ask you. I want to lay things out. I'll tell you my story, then I want an honest answer. You up for this?"

"I don't know. Tell me the story."

"This thing here? This manuscript? This isn't fiction. Maybe it started out to be fiction but this is not fiction. That girl is a real person looking for her mother and that's me."

"You're looking for your birth mother?"

"No way. Hell no. My birth mother died six years ago. She died six years ago."

"Okay, I'm lost. The girl looking for her birth mother is . . . looking for you?"

"You got it, sister," she says, with her old vehemence, punching me lightly on the shoulder.

"Well, so what's the problem? It's not fiction, your daughter is looking for you . . . okay, you imagine this is the letter she's written you. . . ."

"My daughter died when she was born. You get it? She was a stillborn child. Don't you see? You see what I'm driving at?"

"You are imagining a letter written by—"

102

"I ain't imagining nothing, cookie. That girl is alive and she's looking for me. . . ."

"But you just said—"

"She died, I know, I said she died, she was stillborn. . . ."

I experience a dreadful and familiar sinking feeling. It shows up whenever I fear that I have stumbled into something I may not be able to handle. My voice changes, gets stiffer, cooler, more professional. I wish this did not happen but I am not in control of it. "When did you first start to feel that your daughter was looking for you?"

"That one of your shrink questions? Don't pull that stuff on me. . . ."

"Look," I say, brought back to myself by her directness. "I'm totally confused. You bring me a manuscript, you say you want my help writing it. You clearly don't like what you've written and yet you're not ready to throw it out. Now you tell me it's not fiction. Okay, I can work with you on a memoir. But that's not the issue here. You obviously picked me out very carefully because you thought I could answer some question for you. I have a hunch what the question is, but why don't you go ahead and ask it?"

Again, that sense of a violent dislocation in the room, but this time I do not turn to look over my shoulder. I keep my eyes on her and can visibly watch her change. She seems to be shrugging off another protective layer. Sheer vulnerability sits on her face, it alters the appearance of her body, she seems to shrink together and at the same time to be torn open, beyond what is good for anyone, especially in the company of a stranger. I have the distinct sense all this means she is going to risk trusting me and I'm not sure I want her to.

"If I tell you that a daughter is looking for me," she says

tonelessly, "a daughter who died when she was born . . ." Here she stops to shake her head hopelessly. "Can you make sense of that? Can you, without thinking that I am crazy?"

The question, in its raw honesty, its naked risk, cuts to the bone.

"Am I crazy?" she says, in a hoarse voice, leaning close to me. "Am I . . . psy-cho-tic?"

It takes me a moment to find my voice. "Well, to tell you the truth," I say, looking hard for whatever truth might be available, "I find it reassuring that you have put your question in this way. You ask if we can make sense of your experience without prematurely drawing the conclusion that you are mad. Well, why shouldn't we be able to do so? That's what I immediately ask myself. Why shouldn't we look for the meaning of your experience? If we have to draw the conclusion that you're crazy," I hear myself say recklessly, "we can always do that later on. . . ."

The look she directs at me, piercing, suspicious, probing, vulnerable (a strangely robust expression to be carrying so much feeling), gives me the impression that I'm being read and by someone who knows what she's up to. I'd like to shut myself down, close a door, stay hidden, but I know that I'd better bear up to this scrutiny.

"Okay," she says, in a slightly comic drawl, "if you can manage a sense of humor at a time like this. Well, okay. I guess things can't be that bad, after all. . . ."

"They could still be pretty bad," I say. I am thinking hard about Sylvia, whose mother was not dead, although her daughter spoke of her as if she were. Perhaps this confusion of life and death, this uncertainty how the categories might be applied to a dead child or a lost mother is built into the mother-story. "No guarantees, okay? We've said we'll try to figure out an explanation. Sometimes that means knowing how to tell the story. Sometimes . . ."

"Yeah, yeah, and sometimes it means the person, story or not, is just a plain old nut."

The Second Session

Before our next session, I have received two faxes telling me that she is working on the "novel." These communications have, in part, the wry, humorous note we both found comforting during our first meeting. I, however, am warning myself not to be overly reassured by our shared capacity to make light of what troubles us. Madness moves mysteriously, sometimes very slowly, building itself up by degrees from a quirky idea, through a wild thought, to a dangerously established delusion, which may take its way to an extreme, sometimes irreversible state through various disguises, including humor. My task here, the one for which she has deliberately chosen me, is to hold open the possibility that she has an important piece of work to accomplish, which might drive her mad or might instead, if we do this well, save her from madness.

When she arrives, she tells me, even before she sits down at the desk, that she's been able to go on writing because she can now "hear" the voice of the daughter who is looking for her. Hearing voices is, for some people, a bad sign. For others, it is part of the work they have to do.

She sits down heavily at the desk but doesn't push the manuscript around. She has both hands on it, almost protectively, not exactly folded, but somehow, suggestively, as if she had grown fond of this work that is causing her so much distress. She's back in robust mode and I am comforted by this.

"When do you hear the voice?" I ask, tentatively. "When you're writing? As if it were, more or less, dictating to you?" I'm hoping this is the case; it is an experience some writers have and has (or need have) nothing to do with insanity.

"Right before I'm falling asleep. I keep thinking I should wake up to write it down but I can't wake up. So, maybe I'm dreaming. But the next day, when I go over to my computer, the voice just replays itself word for word, as if I had recorded it on a tape machine."

I knew a writer who felt that she was taking down fully formed sentences and ideas. She too used the image of the tape recorder. I am also reminded of Rilke, who heard, from the balcony of Duino Castle, a voice shouting at him through the storm, with the first lines of the *Duino Elegies*. I have always wished it had been possible to ask him what the voice sounded like. Was it male or female? Did it shriek and cry, madly, like the storm? Or did it come with a loud, insistent sense of sober delivery?

Because Rilke died before I was born, and I could not address the question to him, I decide to address it to her, very seriously. This is a tricky decision. I want to help her draw out and elaborate what she might be thinking about this voice. I don't, however, want to give her the impression that I, in asking these questions, am endorsing the voice she hears as that of her daughter, a living person. I explain this distinction to her; she interrupts me.

"Sure sure sure. I get it. You don't want me to think you agree with me that this is my daughter's voice. Okay, I'm game. Sure, sure, sure. I know how to play. You ask the questions, I answer them, this is . . . an ex-er-cise. . . ."

106

Her willingness to "play a game," to "practice an exercise" should reassure me that she is not (not yet, at any rate) in the grip of a delusion. But I am not reassured. Her impatience with the distinction that seems so important to me, her interruption and rough reassurances, remind me that there is something deeply puzzling, troubling, unnerving to her about her conviction that her daughter is alive. This girl, who died at birth, is trying to get hold of her, to reach and communicate with her. I am holding out for a symbolic meaning to an event she is experiencing as real.

Often, in a moment of indecision, when I don't know what to do, I find that I am saying something, taking a direction. Something in me (Is it wise? Is it reckless?) has decided to pursue the line of questioning about the "daughter's" voice.

"Okay then," I say, "in the letter from your daughter, which you have been writing or transcribing, she tries to convince you that she is your long-lost child. Now tell me about the voice you hear. Is it different than what has been written? Tell me, if you can, and tell me very precisely, What does the voice sound like? What can you say about the voice? Or about the person through her voice?"

"Ha, that's a good one," she says, leaning forward to put her elbows on the desk. "That's easy. Young. She is young and she is determined. My daughter . . . I mean that died, I mean . . . and this one, writing to me, would have to be twenty-nine years old. But she sounds . . . the voice sounds . . . younger. Kind of tough, like. Kind of . . . the voice of someone . . . this gal, you know . . . has been, she's been through a lot . . . beaten up . . . survived it. . . ."

"Can you get an impression of the way the person would look who speaks in that voice?"

"That's easy," she repeats, but then has nothing to say. I watch her shrug off her outer protective robust personality. It is an event

I still find shocking for its concrete vividness. The suspicious look shows up. "You having me on?" she says, glaring around the room. She moves about restlessly in her chair, unbuttons her cuff, rolls up the sleeve of her shirt, rolls it down again, buttons it. Then, after a good ten or fifteen minutes, the vulnerable self (raw, wounded, capable of incredible emotional risk) comes up with an answer. She speaks in a husky voice, almost whispered, a lacerated voice. She says: "Like me . . . she looks like me . . . only better. She's done better with her hair."

"Okay," I say, shaking myself out of the fascination Juana holds for me. "You go ahead and picture her, picture her as vividly as you can and hold on to the image. I'm going to read what you've written."

"Nay, nay, nay," she interrupts me after a few sentences. "You can't get it. It's all wrong. Try it like this. . . ."

She closes her eyes and without looking at the manuscript begins to recite, word for word, what she has written on the page. There are no pencil marks and scratchings on these pages. There is very little punctuation, an occasional comma, no periods, the words give the impression of a torrential flow, checked only by an occasional bold dash or highly idiosyncratic quotation mark. They bring before me a young, desperate, tough and determined woman, who reminds me of Juana, or, more precisely, perhaps of what she might have been like at the same age. There is a suggestion, in the rough, wild language, of a hard shell cracking, giving way to sudden moments of vulnerability, raw need, a hope so nearly unbearable it must immediately be reined in and withdrawn.

Juana's recitation is an outpouring that cannot be stopped. Her eyes are closed, she has wrapped her arms around her waist and rocks herself slightly. Or perhaps it would be more accurate to say that she is rocked by the power of language passing through her. I am not certain whether to interrupt her or let her go on; before I can decide, she brings herself back with a violent shudder and stares at me with a look of angry confusion.

"What's been happening here? What's going on?" she asks belligerently.

I tell her about Rilke at Duino Castle. I mention other writers I know who compose in a kind of swept-up state, an inspiration.

"That's what's happening? An in-spir-ation?" She pronounces the word as if it were alien to everything she's ever thought about herself. Then, she glares at me suspiciously. "But that's not all there is to it, is there?"

"You came here to ask me if you are going crazy. Are you going crazy? I don't know. The way we're proceeding is a huge risk. It takes you into unusual mental states, to say the least. But our work presupposes that you can get somewhere useful going on like this. If you can put up with the ambiguity, it's possible that the voice itself will give us some information."

"Is it a risk you'd take?" She says this in the hoarse, vulnerable voice.

"I think I'd have to."

"Have to? Have to? I don't like have to. . . ."

"Well, look. What do we know so far? A young woman is writing to her mother. She gives no details about herself. For pages and pages she seems to cry out to let the mother know how much she needs her. I keep wondering how I would feel if I received such a letter in the mail. How would you feel?"

"I'd be scared to death. I'd think she was some kind of nut or something. I wouldn't have anything to do with her."

"That's the problem, so far, as a piece of writing. This would-be daughter, this stranger, is trying to awaken someone's interest or attention, to get them to notice her, to see she's there. The voice is strident and insistent in the desperation of its need to be heard. It's too intense, too wild, too passionate, in its effort to reach someone. Therefore, it can only drive them away. I think it might be time to acknowledge her."

She has been following this, it seems to me, with all the belligerence, watchfulness and penetration of which she is capable. Then, she seems to get it. "You think I should . . . hey, write back?" she asks with a broad smile, thumping her hand on her knee. "Let her know I've heard?"

She grabs for the pen, ready to begin.

"Go home," I say. "Time's up. I'm exhausted."

She throws a big bear hug around my shoulders. "You said it, sister. You're not the only one. . . ."

Halfway through the room she rushes back and shakes me by my shoulder. "You remind me of my mother. I used to exhaust her too. Only she'd never, ever say so. . . ."

The Third Session

Connection has been made. The "mother" has responded in writing to the "daughter" and the voice Juana hears shouting at her now calms down. It still "talks" during the night and "recites" when Juana sits down at the computer. But now, in place of the desperate plea to be heard, it has started to provide information.

Juana is absorbed in the process of writing, it is difficult to interrupt it to come meet with me. She makes and cancels several sessions. Finally, because I am worried about her, I urge her to make and keep her next appointment. Once here, she seems uninterested in the question of what is happening or whether she's going crazy. I, however, keep trying to figure out what kind of psychological event is taking place for her. I want to trust wherever this story, unfolding at such a remarkable speed, might be taking us, but I also have to make sure that Juana is safe. What kind of standards and considerations should be in place here? I've never come across anything like this before.

She's losing weight, her sleep is interrupted, she writes at an incredible speed and has begun to talk fast. Her mind seems to be racing, trying to keep up with what she is learning about the "history" of the "voice." The layers of personality, tough, wary, sensitive, seem to have been replaced by a hectic, driven, wild-looking woman, whom colleagues of mine would certainly call manic.

Does that mean we should stop, turn back? Should I make a referral? Ger her on medications? Is this a decision I should make?

"Look here," I say, toward the end of our third session, during which she has read to me, in a trembling voice, the "letters" she has been writing to her daughter, letting her know she has "received" her message. "A lot of people would think you're going off the deep end with all this. What do you think?"

"My husband thinks I'm getting worse and worse. He says I should stop seeing you. You know what I say to him? I say, *bullshit!*"

"Not a very respectful way to talk to a husband."

"There you go again," she says with a great roar of laughter. Then, cautiously, with a quick glance over her shoulder, "Are *you* worried about me?"

"Sure. Sure I am. I don't know where all this is going."

"Well," she says, with a triumphant shout, "we'll just have to wait until the story tells us." Her bark of laughter gradually sub-sides. She is now in earnest. "This here is my choice," she says, in a threatening voice. "My choice, mine. This here decision I hand over to no other person. Hey? Not even to you."

"It's your choice, as long as you can tolerate my reminding you of the risks involved."

"My choice," she repeats stubbornly, shaking her head. "You back out, that's your choice. I go on alone."

She glares at me, I shrug my shoulders. She's right. She doesn't have to follow my advice. If I told her to stop now she wouldn't.

So far, the story has told us that the woman writing to her birth mother is twenty-nine years old. She's lived with her adopted family, Seventh-Day Adventists, in the Sacramento Valley, has been taught to attend church regularly, rebelled when she was young and was regularly beaten for it. She never went back to church. She's worked as a waitress since she was thirteen years old, has been having an affair with her boss, a married man, since that time. She doesn't like him but "he's better than nothing." Every night, when she arrives home, she is told to go to her room and to wait for her father to come home from work. When he arrives, he locks the door behind him, takes off his belt and beats her. She has learned not to cry out. She won't give him that comfort. She left home when she was eighteen, moved into town and lived openly with the owner of the restaurant, who had left his wife. He never divorced and they never married. She doesn't like him, she re-peats, but "he's better than nothing." Recently, he has started to drink and that makes her feel she's ready to move on. But where will she go? There is no place for her, unless her mother wants her.

Are these disguised or coded memories from Juana's own childhood? She is sure they are not. Her father was a gentle, passive man, nothing like the macho stereotype of a Chicano. Her mother was the tough one, cold, hard-working. It's because of her mother that she wanted me to understand what it was like not to have money. She wanted me to know how a woman can be driven mean by anxiety about money. She doesn't want me or anyone else to blame her mother. She'd had a hard life, she'd done the best she could and she'd never, ever, of this Juana was certain, ever raised a hand to her.

The Fourth Session

A long, arid period sets in. The "voice" has fallen silent. Juana herself is quiet and depressed. She has to force herself to write, and does so in an effort to tell her daughter that she is not sure she is ready to meet her, there are so many things she hasn't worked out in her own life, she's never worked, she's married to a man with some money whom she doesn't really like (but he's better than nothing). She assures the daughter that she wants the correspondence to continue but it does not.

"She's hurt, isn't she? She's withdrawn, hasn't she? That's what I would do if someone, if my mother, told me she wasn't ready for me yet."

"Pretty lame, if you ask me."

"Meaning what?"

"What does not ready mean? Why aren't you? What are you afraid of?"

"Okay, you want to know? You want to know? Sooner or later she's going to wonder . . . she's going to ask me . . . why . . . I gave her up."

"Well, why did you?"

"But I didn't . . . I mean . . . how could I give her up if she . . . I mean, if she died, I didn't give her up. . . . If I gave her up . . . I mean, hey, what the hell's going on here? What kind of story is this?"

"Well, you're trying to think something it's hard for you to think."

"No shrink stuff for me," she responds quickly.

"Well then, let's wait it out. Let's stick to the material we have so far. A series of letters between mother and daughter. It's wild and torrential and has no form. But good stuff is there. Why don't we start to weed it out and reassemble it?"

"What is it you think I'm trying to think?"

"I was wondering how you were told about your daughter's death."

"How I was told? What do you mean, how was I told? The nurse, the doctor, I don't know. Why? Someone at the hospital must have told me. What are you getting at?"

"It seems to me you have a very considerable doubt about whether you were told the truth."

I've heard of people being "knocked for a loop" but have never witnessed any behavior that matched up with this expression. Juana has just sprawled back in her chair with so much force that her body recoils, her head and neck twist to the right, toward me, while her legs and torso jerk convulsively in the opposite direction, as if she were simultaneously leaning in and running away.

When she recovers herself, she says, hoarsely, with an extreme agitation, "But what if I can't remember? What if I can't? What if I can't?"

"I guess you'd have to make it up. You'd have to imagine, or in-

114

vent it, and maybe in that way you'd come close to some kind of truth."

"That's it. I can't go on. You're just not making any sense. Maybe that's all I can take for now. Invent the truth? That's what you said? I'm beginning to wonder who's crazy. . . ."

She gathers her papers and handbag, taps me on the shoulder as she shuffles past me. "I'll call you," she says dryly, "I'll be in touch. We'll make an appointment. . . ."

"We already have an appointment. Same time, next week."

She cancels the next regular appointment, doesn't show up for the following, is cold, hostile and withdrawn when I call to check in.

"I've dumped the whole thing," she says.

"Dumped it? Actually thrown it out?"

"Yeah, well. I've got it on the computer."

A silence. We both hang on to our fraying connection, neither able to put down the phone. It's her choice, of course, if she's decided not to go on, if the whole thing has become too much for her.

"You think someone lied to me? Is that what you're driving at? You think my daughter never died but someone told me she died?"

"There is no way for me to know that. We're talking about something that happened twenty-nine years ago. I never knew these people. But I certainly have the impression you are wondering if a lie was told."

"My mother," she says, after a tense silence, "was capable of almost anything. Almost anything if it was good for her family. I was sixteen years old, pregnant, the guy had run off, I refused to have an abortion. We fought about it every day, screaming and shouting, until it was too late. But she kept on pestering and insulting. 'This is the life your father and I slaved to give you? Your life is over if you go on like this. What kind of life are you going to have? High school dropout, poor, single, estranged from your family?' It wasn't shame about sex or anything like that. It was her grim, I mean grim and hard and cruel, sense of life. But I wouldn't let her overpower me. That was her view. She saw me going under. Right down into the gutter, she said. But I saw differently, I thought I could make it, I wanted to have that kid, or maybe I just wanted to stand up to my mother. . . ."

"So, she was capable of almost anything," I say after a long silence.

"What are you driving at?" she shouts back at me and slams down the phone.

A minute later she calls back. "I don't think she was capable of that," she says and hangs up again.

This time weeks go by before I hear from her. One day a fax arrives asking if she can still have her regular appointment. I fax back that she can. The morning of our session she leaves two messages telling me she wants me to read something before we meet and will fax it over. The fax, when it arrives, is a single piece of paper with three hand-written lines, heavily underlined.

IF SHE WAS CAPABLE OF THAT

I WOULDN'T BE CRAZY

WOULD I?

I stand by the fax machine staring at this paper. If her mother was capable of giving the baby up for adoption and telling her that the baby had died, the daughter would not be crazy when she insists her child is alive. Was her mother capable of this lie? This is, perhaps, the forbidden thought that has been trying to make its way through. The wild writing, the torrential flow of words, the insistent sense that a dead daughter is in fact alive—these may have been her effort to think something unthinkable about her mother. If so, it may be this unthinkable thought that will allow her to give birth to a new understanding of her mother, her motivations, her capacity to take control of her daughter's life, to impose her will, tyrannically, upon another person's destiny. The mother capable of this, the mother Juana has never been able to imagine, whom she has tried to protect from her own critical thoughts and from other people's censure, probably has to be conceived and given form if Juana is to free herself from a dangerous obsession. Then, perhaps, she can take steps to find the daughter who may be alive. I cannot get my eyes off this single page. The possibilities, here, of giving birth to a mother multiply dramatically. If Juana dares to think through this forbidden thought about her own mother, she may then be free to imagine herself a mother of a living child, who may in turn someday be reunited with her birth mother.

The Fifth Session

The woman who shows up for our fifth session has changed in several ways from the woman who originally came to speak with me. She is thinner, more subdued, she has cut her hair very short. She reminds me of women whose heads were shaved during the war for having had sex with the enemy, or of a nun, cutting her hair to take the veil, or of a woman sacrificing her luxurious, curly locks in an act of penance.

"We'll never know, will we?" she asks tonelessly, staring at her hands.

"There's no one to ask? No one who might have some information?"

"Would she dare to tell anyone something like that? Not my father. He was a quiet man but he would have killed her. I just know it. Or maybe that's what I have to think. He would have killed her. He's dead, there's her sister . . . would she have told her? Told her sister? Nay, nay, nay . . . never. She's old now, mostly she drifts off, somehow I can't imagine asking her." Still, she seems cheered by the thought. "Hey there, Aunt Seria, remember me? Rowena's daughter? You know that baby I had that died? You think Mom might have given her up for adoption?"

Her body starts to shake, first her hands, then her shoulders, while she bends over to press her face against her knees. "She was my mother. My mother." She waits. "How could a mother do something like that to her own daughter?"

She makes an odd barking sound, which could be laughter or tears or something else entirely, a shudder of horror, a gasp of comprehension. I put my hand on her shoulder. "Yeah," she says, "good. Keep it there." A while later she says, in a muffled voice, "It's a kind of love, isn't it? If you think of it like that? A cruel kind of love?" She lifts her head; her face is pale but composed, except for a slight twitch at the corner of her mouth. "She was doing it for me. She would have believed that. And then she would have to live her whole life, the whole rest of it, choking that lie. And all for my sake . . . that's what she would have been telling herself . . . all for my sake. Would she be capable of that? We know, don't we? For me, for the better life she wanted me to have. She would have been capable of . . . anything . . ."

118

*   *   *

That session, our last regular meeting, took place several months ago. Since then, Juana has sent me reports about her investigation and has come in a few times, "just to set eyes on me." She's hired an attorney, secured her husband's cooperation, and has developed inventive ways to look for a child who might have been given up for adoption twenty-nine years before, and who might, or might not, be looking for her birth mother or have been raised in a Fundamentalist family. The voice has fallen silent. It did not survive the emergence of the unthinkable thought about Juana's mother. The manuscript has been "tucked up somewhere safe," in case Juana ever wants to return to it. "There's work to be done here," she says, "channels created to help people locate each other. It's like a war, it's like we've been through a war and been separated and have to find each other again. Everyone needs help starting out, figuring out what might have happened. It's a god-awful process. Awful, just awful. All that waiting, the false hopes, the wrong leads. Sometimes you're just sure you've been lying to yourself, throwing out money, spending all your time for nothing substantial. It ruins families, it destroys life, something nothing comes of it. It's usually mothers and daughters, that's my impression, who keep trying to find each other, against all the odds. It keeps me going. I sit at my desk. I think of all this desperate love out there trying to locate someone who might belong to you. . . . How could I stop?"

I heard this story last summer, when I was visiting a friend in Tuscany. Instantly, I resolved to make it part of my collection, for its ability to detect beneath the serene surface of the conventional, the turbulent, often hidden undercurrents of the mother-daughter bond. The storyteller, a woman in her late forties, seemed to be unearthing unexpected structures of meaning as she talked, as if she were participating in her own archeological dig. She had come to my friend's house for dinner, bringing olive oil and wine she had produced on the small farm where she spent summers and vacations. I spent a single night with her, while my friend was busy on the telephone with one of her kids who was in crisis. The story, however, has continued to fascinate me for the way it descends, step by step, into its often unsuspected daughter-guilt and anguish.

WHAT BEATRICE SAID

Ecco, okay, here goes, I begin. But is there something worthwhile to this story? It has no madness, no abuse, no divorce, no alcoholism, no angry fighting between parents behind locked doors. This is a story about the archetypal, normal, happy family. Two parents, both very attractive people, mother tall and pretty, father good-looking, both involved in sports and the good life of the bourgeoisie, with the discreet charm of it raised to a high art by my mother's social ambitions. There are also three little daughters, absolutely perfect little girls, groomed into dolls with curls and ribbons. These girls are of course never dirty and never impolite; they have the very best manners which charm the parents of all their friends, so that of course all their friends are envious of them, and also all the grown-up people who see this little family are very envious and jealous and in high admiration of them, because they are so happy and so normal and so perfect. They live in this little house just outside of Florence, up in the hills, and the father makes a nice living because he is a dentist and after the war and the hard times and the bad nutrition there is plenty of work for him. He's quite chic because he has a car, and my mother is determined after a tumultuous youth and the war that she will create an absolute safe haven where everything is straight and right and happy and pink. And very, very clean. She had grown up in a family with Socialist parents, lived through the Depression, her father was arrested as a political prisoner in the Mussolini time, and out of all that she became a person with iron energy and an iron will, an absolutely unbelievable willpower. She pushed her husband to work harder and make more money, she saved by preparing three meals a day for everyone, she did the accounting for his business and supervised the children's homework. She had taught them to read and write before they started school because they were going to be model children, so that her family and everything about them would mirror back to her the success of her enterprise. You can admire my mother and you can have sympathy for her and I do admire her. But this woman of iron will is not an easy woman to have for a mother.

I am a painter, I paint miniature scenes, but while I am painting I am talking to myself, telling myself stories that come out in
shapes and images and colors. Whereas my mother is this person
who has such big feelings that she never finds words or images or
any expression for them. This is a big difference between us, it always was a big difference and it created conflict. It's as though my
mother is a . . . a wine-skin that has to burst under the pressure of
her feelings. They don't and they can't and they won't find a verbal
outlet. Maybe she wants you to know what these huge feelings are
without having to be told. Maybe the feelings are too large for
words, or maybe she never had sufficient practice to put them into
words. So, these feelings that can't be expressed come out as terrible moods, they create an atmosphere of profound need, anguish,
disapproval, longing. A sad, sad longing, as if you have let her
down in some way. And then withdrawal. For a child it is very
hard to live with these silent moods. There is coldness, absence,
withdrawal of love. When I was little and I had done something,
or when I was a teenager and had done something wrong, she
could fall silent, completely silent, and not address me for days on
end, until I could not stand it anymore. There was no limit to
what she could stand of her own coldness, and the complete cutting me off. And only if I came verbally back to her on my knees
saying, "I'm so sorry, I have sinned, I've done this to you and I'll
never, never do it again," that was the magical formula that had to
be said. Then she was the real mother again, she was the good
mother again, the loving, caring monkey-mother. The mother
you can cling to, who never lets go of you, the mother who holds
on and you hold on to her through everything. If you have a monkey-mother, who really is a good mother when she's like that, you
won't be able to tolerate the withdrawal. You'll do anything to

please her, you are in her power, this mother is going to have an incredible power over her children.

Let's say you do something wrong. You are a little child and you . . . well, suppose I dirty myself, spill something over myself. I had a terrible fear of being dirty, not in the metaphorical sense, but just in a very concrete sense. Peeing in my pants or shitting in my pants when I didn't get to the bathroom in time. Of incurring her wrath by being too loud, too excited. The best example is . . . I think it symbolically probably impressed me very much. Remember, we are back in the poor and black market-ridden times of Italy in the first months after the war. Or maybe it was a little later, when a few things were finally coming back into the city—and somebody, a friend of my parents perhaps, had brought us a block of chocolate. Not a tablet, you know, chocolate for cooking, to be melted. It was the first time my sisters and I had seen chocolate. So my parents and their friends who brought this gift were sitting at the table at dinner and having a great time, and my sisters and I were behind the stove, melting bits of chocolate and forming little figures and animals and at some point we had the great inspiration to stretch out our chocolate covered hands from behind the oven and shout, "black market, black market."

I think probably the company laughed and found it extremely funny, but we must have got the chocolate over our clothes as well, and my mother got furious. In the middle of all that company she got furious, she took the chocolate dolls and whatever was left of the block and threw them into the oven, completely beside herself in a rage. In front of everybody. And we were horribly ashamed, because we also believed in our perfect family and this rage was in front of company and that was truly horrifying. I was maybe four or five years old but the craziness of the act was very clear to me, that such a precious, precious gift would land in the oven because my mother was in a rage because she couldn't control us.

The fact that my mother had to destroy a creative outlet for me and my sisters was, I think, part of the story, it was very significant or at least later on it became significant. This could be confusing. Because at the time my mother was the kind of mother who let her little girls putter and make and do things from morning to night. I think she was very relieved that we could be such good company to each other and this was also her image of the perfect family. She would of course sew and knit and crochet and embroider and cook and bake and cut out paper dolls for us—she was very handy and she would do with us everything that a child could want to do. We had a dollhouse, we had a little shop, we had just all these wonderful, magical toys, which she made. So in one sense you would say she was very creative, but these things were an occupation for her and for us, all elements of beautifying the house, decorating it, being useful, occupying time. The fact that creativity could have another purpose and another end was totally alien to her. In some way it disturbed her, it frightened her, it unsettled her.

I knew very early on that there were many things I could never tell her. It was absolutely impossible. From almost the moment I had consciousness and memory, from age four or five, I knew that my mother was good at making and doing things and you could ask her for help with anything practical. But there were other things, which were the most difficult and painful things in my life, that I could not discuss with her. For instance, the fact that kids my age didn't understand me, that my experience seemed to be different from theirs, that I was lonely or lived somewhat in a different realm. Probably my whole magical belief in angels and God and somehow the romantic elements in nature, fairy tales and mystical stories—these things meant so much to me and they meant nothing to my mother and I knew this. I was alone with them, I somehow felt that they were embedded in another universe that she just simply had no access to, but that it was the true world, the real world where I breathed and lived day by day by day and that to some degree I probably shared with my sisters. To some degree; because we would paint these angels endlessly and draw them and cut them out and fantasize about them.

My mother had the good sense to keep my drawings. And she collected my first little comic strips and stuff like that. And she also certainly gave me some applause for that. But very early I had the feeling that she couldn't judge them. She didn't know what to make of them, which is very bad for a child. It leaves behind a feeling you cannot name at the time, but which I now still remember and I now would call it guilt. Something that aches and squeezes you inside you and makes you want to run to your mother to comfort her . . . for . . . for what? For not knowing things you already know. You are only a little child, but you know things your mother just can't grasp. You feel so sad for her, and then you want to do something to make up to her. That is the beginning of something very dangerous for a daughter, the beginning of the way you start to lose yourself, to give up yourself to join in with your mother. You don't want to be better than she is at anything, especially not better than this woman who is so proud at being so good at what she does. It was a relief to me that my mother collected my drawings and paintings because she saw they could make an impression on her friends. So in a way making them became a way to give her something, I gave her something to be proud of, to show off with. "Look at my daughter! Look what she's done!"

But underneath this was a lonely feeling, a terrible and lonely feeling. Because she couldn't see me; she simply didn't see me and couldn't know me and my real life was apart from her.

That is bad because it involves a constant distortion of the self. The monkey-mother grooms the monkey-daughter constantly, there is not one detail that escapes the mother, not a curl of it doesn't sit right, or a ribbon that doesn't sit right, or a politeness that is lacking, or the manners at table. There was the extreme femininity that she imposed on her girls, always being dressed the same, so we were the perfect feminine exhibition pieces of my mother's value, and what she stood for and wanted to stand for, and we had to perform that perfect femininity for everybody to see. So, being seen was absolutely the crucial element in my mother's worldview. And there we were, or rather there I was—I don't know how much my sisters shared any of this—but there I was, feeling that I was dissected, criticized, picked upon, glorified when I performed, and at the same time, never, never, never seen. That was a very big dilemma, because my mother was very appealing in her monkey-mother behavior, she made you feel unbelievably safe, she was a rock of safety and good judgment, you could totally rely on her. And whenever things in this narrow, restricted world of hers were difficult, you could always go to her and she would put an arm around you and take the thing away. She could, in her terrain, always give you the feeling that everything was *bene, molto bene,* because Mother is there.

It is very seductive. She can tell you what a child needs to hear and wants to hear and then you just go on, you don't solve anything and you don't get real help or understanding, but there is always the feeling that you're not alone—even though you are, completely, completely alone.

This maybe, here, right here, is the story worth telling. Beneath all this creation of the ideal daughter of the loving mother of the perfect family, another self is growing up very unhappy in the daughter and not seen and not known or understood and one day the unhappiness of this hidden self comes all out onto the surface.

This happened, with us, at age sixteen.

I found a friend, she became my real passion, my first real friend, her name was Gabriella, I called her Abra, which always infuriated my mother because she was, maybe, the first person who came between us. I had a girlfriend, a whole separate realm, where I could be enthusiastic, could have the most crazy, romantic, infantile or absurd feelings that were taken for granted by her. Everything my mother never recognized and didn't like I could do and express with Abra. I spent my days trotting through town with Abra and even sleeping over. Abra's family was, well, impossible, from my mother's point of view . . . the mother divorced, giving the daughter perfect freedom, letting her wear jeans, letting her smoke and boys could come over and even stay overnight.

In this same time I had also met a friend who was ten years older and a painter. His name was Paolo, which he changed to Pavel, because it sounded like a more artistic, avant-garde name to him. He was part of an elite existentialist artist group that was interested in everything foreign, and especially Russian and German and French. So he now all of a sudden opened wide these doors to culture and art, at the very highest standard. And I would study and read voraciously practically everything he gave me and everything I could find, in terms of art and literature. He took me to avant-garde galleries and openings. In Florence, of course, you go to museums in every class in every year of school, but this was different. I didn't understand the paintings but Paolo made me look at them for hours and they began to feel a part of me.

Of course, because I was still only sixteen years old, I had this naive desire to share all this world with my mother, who of course was still claiming to be the best friend of her daughters. But now somehow this didn't work. My mother tried, quite bravely for a number of years, and then she completely gave up. She couldn't keep up with us. She tried to understand the futurists, Kandinsky, Dada. You name it, anything that was important in those years, in the late fifties. That's what she did. My mother. This is really a sad story, because she tried to keep up with us but how could she keep up with us when all she knew was the little perfect world she had created in which there was nothing dark or dirty or noir. I don't like to be cruel, but I always get this absurd picture of my mother sitting with her arms pressed against her body to keep her elbows from flying up, the way she taught us when we were children, and meanwhile she is trying to read about the art of Francis Bacon. This is the sort of scene I paint but, of course, this I would never paint, it would just break my heart and at the same time, telling about it, I'm laughing. No, I'm crying. No, I don't know what I'm doing, laughing, crying . . .

My mother was so unhappy with this modern art. She didn't understand it and she didn't like it. The bleak worldview that was expressed in it was profoundly against her nature and she didn't want to have anything to do with it.

That is how little by little I lost my mother or she lost me. The old bond withered away. My life was with Abra and Paff, which is what he called himself now, which also infuriated my mother, because she thought he was heading for a nihilist, terrorist future. There was no longer a happy life in our perfect happy family.

Not that the new life was a happy life for me. For me, it was a very divided life. Divided from my mother, and divided also within the new friendships. With Abra I could be wild and silly and funny and always had something absurd to say, and some wild game to play, and we could laugh until we fell on the floor, or sit up listening all night to Renata Tebaldi and crying our eyes out and putting on wigs and makeup and singing whole arias. And this is very interesting because I was always in the role of the man, the young lover, the *enamorato* who will of course have to kill himself in despair when he loses his love. But with Paff and his circle, everything I did was very stilted and horribly self-conscious, as if I was trying to make myself up. My language absolutely seemed to vanish. I had no language to talk to them. It was like being under my mother's surveillance again only now it was intellectual manners and cultural behaviors that mattered. I think I blamed my mother for not preparing me for this life of culture and ideas.

Because I felt that a protected, bourgeois youth was no material for art or drawing, and I thought Paff and his friends were right and I would have to go into all the hell that I could find and reach in order to gain the substance that an artist has to have. Here, too, I blamed my mother. Having been protected by her careful, pink, monkey-family world had been my curse, and now I wouldn't protect myself from anything. Therefore, full masochism, full-blown suffering, horrible sex, abortions, horrible drugs, horrible everything that I could get my hands on, in order to shape myself into a mature person, a mature woman, a real artist. But I didn't make it, not in their eyes. Instead, being a woman in their circle meant becoming the muse, the silent muse, giving in, letting Paff and his artist friends take over my mother's role, even though the setting was so different. I became the object of beauty that they needed for inspiration and liked to display, but there was no possibility of partnership.

Suddenly Paff paints me, I'm his only subject, I'm sitting day and night posing for Paff. So of course he now cannot stand, he really cannot stand, that I am making my little cartoons and drawing and sometimes showing my drawings to his friends. So there we were again, after my mother not being able to tolerate who I was, there was Paff who couldn't tolerate who I was, and the whole thing happened over again. What really mattered to me about my self went underground, everything dreamy and mystical and spiritual and longing for its artistic expression just disappeared. I think I chose him as a real copy of my mother, who was as picky and intolerant and unable to let me be. But of course he was a man, and I was learning from him too, because he had so many interesting tools of art, language, culture and philosophy that I needed and didn't have.

I now saw my mother from a critical distance where I scorned her, where I thought, She is a poor bourgeois nothing, an empty woman who doesn't know anything, who lives a life of convention, who has nothing of her own, who is trapped and will never get out. Trapped by being a mother, being married, being in this kind of conventional lifestyle where show was everything and substance nothing. She didn't have the capacity for anything else, that's how I saw her, and of course Paff and his friends helped with this view and I despised her. And at the same time, I had unbelievable pity for her. It broke my heart to see her like that. Here come those tears again. Here they come. I felt, in my own life, that everything was open to me, like I had everything, all the channels open, not that it was easy, but I discovered that for me life had profound meaning, and the search for meaning and the self was what made my life.

My mother was worried about her oldest daughter. Because I was storming out into a really dark and dangerous world with Paff and drugs and alcohol and some flirting we did with terrorist ideas, and maybe, sometimes, more than flirting. Lesbianism was also lurking there through Abra. My mother wanted to hold on to me because I think, more and more, out of pity and guilt I became the person who tried to save her and give her a new life. I became her partner, I seemed to take my father's place in talking about life. He didn't talk about anything but money and cars and sports. My younger sisters had nothing in their heads but boyfriends and getting married to a rich man, and for some reason they wouldn't say anything about this to me or to my mother. Maybe we hated my mother because of all that control and criticism, so now my sisters found a way to pay her back, to not tell her the very things my mother would have wanted to know.

I, of course, found that what my mother had to say about my affairs was pat, it was always, "Oh, just wait, my dear. You just have to wait for the right man to come." She couldn't understand or follow any spiritual torment and despair with the world. I would, nevertheless, bring her my sorrows. I felt that was the emotional food she needed to subsist on, to keep herself from feeling empty. But at the same time, more and more I had the impression that when I did that, and talked to her about what really went on in my universe and in my soul, that it fell into nothing. It became nothing, just sand, running through my fingers, because she couldn't take it up, she couldn't give me anything back, and I ended up completely empty, the way she was. Somehow, she had swallowed up the despair and left me nothing. She had become the black-hole mother, a terrible, terrible emptiness into which all the emotion you poured was sucked up and never returned and that was the mother of all my later teenage years, until I don't know for how long, maybe forever, one could say. Always a sense that I had to feed my soul to my mother, who needed to feed off it like a vampire. Husband silent and absent, two daughters running about and keeping secrets. I was the replacement partner for her. I had become her husband. And she courted me in some way, and I was extremely important to her.

It's strange, really, how her perfect, picture-book, monkey-daughter had become such a troubled person. I probably was troubled by a profound loneliness, in not having found my artistic expression and wanting to find it and not feeling up to the level of Paff and his friends, and not having, not really ever having Abra, who suddenly didn't have any time for me. I had my daily little drawings, excessive and obsessive comic strips of my life. But these, of course, could not stand up to the scrutiny of Paff and his avant-garde friends. To be at one with them you had to find a grand artistic form, because they were painters and musicians and sculptors and I desperately wanted that, and had the feeling that I either had nothing to say, or didn't have the right form to say it, because when I tried to do "art," out would always come something naive, childlike, with too much romantic enthusiasm or too much despair, which I could never make ironic, which was the correct fashion in that time.

It's funny, when you tell a story and all these random, chaotic pieces fall together. I never thought about how much my relationship with my mother was actually the one consistent thread that ran through my whole life. My sisters went off into marriage and children, Abra came and went and came back and dropped me again, eventually I broke with Paff, who absurdly joined the Communist party. But my mother is always there. At first, I am her monkey-puppet, her little dream doll. Then I become her Pygmalion, with all the contempt that expresses. Next, she's my damsel in distress, the unhappy princess, the forsaken one I am trying to save. Soon, she's turned into my vampire mother, I'm pouring out my soul trying to feed her. Or maybe, to be kinder, you could say this very powerful woman of iron will has become my *mater dolorosa*, standing weeping at the foot of the cross of her failed family ideals, if, pardon me, that image is not too romantic for you. I suppose I could paint her like that, without the cross of course. I myself in the role of the beloved disciple Giovanni, against whom she is leaning, half-fainting, half in agony of silenced protest.

All this entanglement . . . it needs a huge word, something more than attachment, because the bond just holds and holds and can't end and won't end even after she dies, it just won't be broken, it is so passionate. Even when it shatters it is still there, it just takes a different form. That's what I'll tell you now.

I finally decided to leave Italy. I moved to London and became very successful as an organizer of art exhibits and then as an illustrator and finally a painter myself. Really, very successful. So, in a sense, although I almost never saw her during those years, I made my truce—not my peace, but my truce—with my mother. When we met, I was always working very hard to give us the illusion of closeness. I was safe now, I wasn't afraid of losing myself in her, I had a world apart from her. I would always bring things to read and show them and my mother and I would pretend to be best of friends again. And soon, everything ended up on her coffee table, she couldn't resist being proud of me for being successful, even in a world she didn't respect. She relished the fact that her daughter was somebody, even if she was painting things my mother didn't like to look at. She could show off with me again, even though it was uncomfortable too. But what never changed was the black-hole feeling I had about my mother. That she needed me even more than ever because both my sisters had really drifted away and I began to feel that I would never, ever be able to satisfy my mother, no matter how many times I went to visit, or how many trips I agreed to take with them. She was getting older and I could feel her lonely, lonely despair with her life, growing and growing.

It's the look she would give me. The look of a beaten and abandoned dog. It is the look that tells you the dog is completely in love with you, wants to lie at your feet, lie under your feet, is completely dependent on you and in need of you and if you scratch its head or have a kind word for it, well, you've made its day and it will want more. This is something I haven't wanted to paint, you know, but I always see it in my mind. The dog lying at the daughter's feet, but on the animal's head is the mother's face, filled with sorrow and reproach. I wish I could paint it. I don't know if I could paint it. I would never paint it. The creaturelike reproach. It is bad in a dog but in a human face it is even worse, because there's always the remainder of "all the things I've done for you, and look what you do for me, you don't even take the trouble to scratch my ears."

How could you paint something like that, which was not angry, not bitter, filled maybe even with a kind of love that is all mixed up with anguish and agony for the mother? But somehow

135

in the painting you have to show in the dog's human face that the mother needs to seize on your whole soul, nothing else will do to fill the emptiness. This utter despair and passion and sappiness and teariness and neediness has to be in the face. Hunger. What terrible mother-hunger.

I always imagine another painting, which has the mother and daughter standing at the door to say good-bye. It would have to show the way the mother grabs you when she says good-bye and she stares at you with that look. She penetrates you with that look and won't let go. You have to smash a kiss on her just to get away from these eyes. And then you run and run and run. But if this was a painting you would have to show everything at the same time, the mother's look, the agony, the horror and rage the daughter feels, and the running away, everything would have to be present in that angry kiss, that tormented, reluctant, demanded kiss the daughter is just about to bestow on the mother. . . .

Once, toward the end of a visit, my lover had a call from London and we thought we should get back a day or two early. We were having a quiet evening, so I called my mother over and said, "I'll have to be going back a couple of days early to London. Such and such happened and we're really sorry, but it seems like we really should get back."

Well, of course, Mother is immediately, profoundly pissed, deeply wounded and offended. "You can't even give us a week out of your life? You can't show any care or concern for us? If you are in such a hurry, why don't you go tonight?"

My mother was absolutely devastated. All was lost to her. "It's always like this," she says. "You promise and you take away and that is how you have always been. Selfish. Putting yourself first."

She says, "This is the same as last time. You always promise and you never give." I couldn't remember what last time she was talking about and maybe she was right, maybe I left early that time too. "You don't even once have a week for us, not even a week." And so I said, "Well, we always come to this point." I said, pretty much in pain and anger, "There is no understanding between our points of view; I don't get yours, and you don't get mine." And I rose up and left the room.

When I left we hadn't patched anything up. It was a horrible good-bye. My mother looked at me again, teary-eyed and dog-beaten and all of that, with this horrendous-feeling "How can you let me suffer like this?" So then I was in agony. We drove back to London but at the first tank station I got out of the car to go to use the toilet and I was going to call her. I wanted to patch it up, kneel and say I'll never do it again, forgive me, I'll never leave early, I'll come back, I'll catch a train and be there in an hour. My lover stopped me. Then he did something really remarkable. He bought me a large notepad from the store, sort of pushed me into the back seat of the car and started driving, very, very carefully, in the slow lane. I then started drawing like a maniac, the same little cartoon kind of drawings I used to do in my teens.

When we stopped for petrol I showed him these crazy drawings and there were pages full, practically the whole large notepad. So we bought another and I kept on, talking out loud to myself in the back seat, telling myself these weird stories that came out in images. *Aspetto, aspetto,* wait, wait, wait, I'll describe them later. Of course I didn't know it at the time but I was drawing my way out of my mother's tyranny of her sorrow and her empty life and I began to ask myself why there was all this tragedy because I had left my parent's house a day or two earlier than planned.

This is a question of guilt, daughter-guilt. Language cannot describe guilt. It feels like an intense pain, like the heart bleeding. It is so easy to put myself into my mother's place, to see those eyes, and her old age, and to know how she is soon going to die. I can hear all those reproaches and "you never do anything for us" and "not even a week once in a lifetime" and all of that. And it feels like, it makes you feel like the worst criminal, like a loveless beast, completely devoid of love, egoistic, narcissistic, a sick, sick person, who has no drop of normal feelings and doesn't deserve to live.

When we got back to London and looked at all the little cartoon drawings I realized that I had been sketching the individual parts of a huge canvas. How would you paint guilt? The condemned daughter mounting the steps to the guillotine and feeling that she deserves her fate? All around her the crowd is jeering, they're throwing rotten food, people try to break through to pluck at her, to tear at her clothes, to tear out her hair. And on her face this expression of anguished certainty, of deserving exactly the punishment she is about to receive. But the crowd has animal faces and bird faces and reptile faces and of course there is no mother in this painting because the whole painting is a portrait of the mother and only the daughter, in the whole painting, has a tormented human face.

So there I am, I am in a frenzy of painting in my studio in London, with these waves of guilty feeling, and I begin to feel that something in me refuses the responsibility of satisfying my mother by giving her my life blood. I just no longer wanted the role of filling this black hole of her needs.

Then I got stuck. I couldn't go on with my painting. It was sketched in, the crowd figures were there and the daughter climbing up the steps of the guillotine, but suddenly I couldn't go on. All this is of course very dramatic, because when a daughter starts to break with her mother there is going to be one big storm. For days I'm sitting at my window, not eating, not sleeping, and suddenly my lover comes in and says that he noticed something when we talked about leaving my parents' house early, and my mother rejected any kind of change in plan, any idea and compromise, you know, that we would come back earlier at Christmas, or whatever; my lover noticed that my mother didn't have the air of suffering at all, that she was simply in her pester mood: angry, furious, disgusted, indignant, and that only I was suffering, that I was intensely suffering, and that he could read that in my face. My lover could read that in my face.

That was an unbelievable enlightenment for me. I saw that my mother's suffering—I saw it for the very first time—her suffering was a petulance. If she did not get what she wants and what she claims she's entitled to, she believes that she is involved in a mythical, tragical lack of love that is being forced upon her. A knife goes into her heart, is what she claims—a mythical knife—and she has tyrannized the whole family and especially she has tyrannized me with this for all our lives. She made a life out of this suffering.

But what is so tragical about her life? I now started wondering. What's the tragedy? She has a very full, rich and good life, according to her own values. My father has been successful in his business, they move in the highest society, my mother is highly respected, a queen of the provinces, you could say. They have enough money for a comfortable retirement, they travel whenever they want. So why is she so pitiable, in her own eyes?

That was the revelation. She would survive my leaving home

two days early. What a revelation. After that, I never finished my guillotine painting. I just left it there, blocked in, with some smudges of color, and one night I suddenly began to draw eggs. These huge eggs in which you could see other eggs, as if the eggs were pregnant with themselves, and growing bigger, and breaking open and giving birth to eggs that gave birth to eggs and I was in fits of laughter, although I had no idea what I was painting, I just couldn't stop laughing. I was, really, in that time, completely a maniac, telling stories to myself, laughing out loud and painting eggs. Then one early morning suddenly I was done. And I heard myself say—and this is very funny in Italian, but I don't know how it will be in English—I heard myself say, *The shattering of the symbiotic egg.* And that was the name for my series of egg paintings, which of course have no special meaning for anyone else, but for me they meant I was painting out of myself the terrible, unquenchable longing for eternal symbiosis and togetherness with my mother.

During all this time after I left her house two days early, it was as if an ice-time had broken out between my mother and me. Everything froze. Our relationship froze, there was no more love, no more affection, no more tenderness. She had done exactly what she had always done in order to force me onto my knees: turn her back and be cold. But this time I didn't come and say, "I'm so sorry." I confronted her and sent her letters saying, "If you want to go on like this it's fine with me."

She didn't get what she wanted. For once, for once, she could not control me inside my own feelings, she could not wring me with guilt. The daughter was never, ever going up the stairs to the guillotine. And this became in myself and in her too a landslide. The whole landscape of our relationship changed. It was very unpleasant to be in the ice, of course, but the air was crisp and clear and the distance created by it felt healthy and normal. There shouldn't be this exaggerated closeness and warmth, which was always only our totally infantile desire for perfect union. There was always something artificial about it. And it shouldn't be there, and I shouldn't have been trying to create it because there is no reason to be enthusiastic about our togetherness. We are just very ordinary folk when we get together now, we are talking for two minutes at a time and having nothing to say anymore, but tolerating this and hanging out if things are okay, watching television, doing basically, really nothing. And it's very boring and also very peaceful and quite sweet, and it's just, that's how my parents' life is. And that's all.

It all ended with the shattering of the eggs. My own nostalgic connection to Mother, my little child's hunger for a mother who would really be there, and could be worshiped and really loved, and could recognize me. I never had that mother, and here was the dream of her finally shattered with the breaking of the eggs.

Because of course, from out of the ice, over time, there grew out a simple landscape of dust and some green trees and a little shrubbery, nothing splendid, but nothing really horrible either, you know. A populated desert, I would call it, of our old connection, that allowed me to be different, because now I'm not trying to save her, I'm not anymore trying to bring her to life. I'm not doing anything. I'm just accepting things as they are. And I can do that.

Well, maybe one thing to add is that in some extremely funny way, ironic way, it seems to be a relief to my mother. The whole story from age sixteen had just come to an end. I had put her under this incredible demand of having to be somebody she wasn't, just as she had always put the same demand on me. I didn't want to be her perfectly feminine bourgeois daughter marrying a wealthy man. And she could never become a bleak, passionate, despairing intellectual. And now that I am not doing this anymore, you know, demanding anything or coming up with topics or conversations and talks and books to try to bridge the gap between us, now that I'm not doing anything, she's much more relaxed, and she can be a little bit herself.

After all these years of thinking that she was trying to change me, I've realized that I've been just as intolerant of her. Now, accepting the reality of who she is, the difference between us, the unbridgeable gulf between our lives, makes me believe that her life—although it's totally empty according to my values—is not empty for her. I don't even know that she feels so empty. Wouldn't it be funny if all along my mother was just iron-willed and stubborn and wanted me to do things her way and would use guilt to punish me if I didn't? And that was all there was to it? And all I had to do was shrug it off and go my own way, which in fact I did? And what is all that tragedy and agony and suffering? It was there, but there was no real reason for it. Is that what it comes down to in the end? Is that the answer to the question you asked me? Did I give birth to my own mother? How did I give birth to her? Well, that's how. . . .

11

·

STACEY'S STORY

"Hi, this is Stacey. Remember me? My mother wants to come in with me. Call me if it's okay. Same number. I'm back in town. Boy, she wants to come in with me. She wants to come in. So, I'm scared, you better believe it, but I'm glad it's going to happen."

She had left town after a relatively short period of work with me to accept a scholarship to a graduate school on the East Coast. For several months, after her departure, she called once a week with a brief message to tell me she was doing well. In time, the calls became less frequent, dwindled to once a month or so, fell off. This fast-paced message, which seemed to pick up our work where we had left off, was the first time I had heard her voice in years. Nevertheless, I recognized it instantly and felt that I too had been waiting for the continuation of our conversations.

A second message came the same day before I had a chance to call back. "This is Stacey. Remember me? So, I promised to call if my mother agreed to come in. Well she has and so I did and it's like I've never even been away. It's like I've been waiting all these years for her to say yes. She's said yes. Can you believe it? But the thing is, should I come in first alone? But if we wait, you know, she might just change her mind, so I'm not sure what to do or even if your offer is still good and you're willing to work with us."

I called back to offer an appointment for the next day, a Friday, my day off. I left it to her whether she wanted to come in alone or bring her mother. "Hey, yeah, sure I'd like to catch up after all these years but really, with Mother and me, nothing has changed. We're right back where we were so I thought we might as well jump in and pick it up from there now that she's agreed. She's agreed. Can you believe it? But now that she has I'm really scared. Like, what am I going to say? Okay, I guess I'll come in first and then the three of us can meet together."

We arranged for her to come in the next day alone. I suggested I call her mother to introduce myself and to find out if she wanted an appointment of her own before the three of us met together. I was curious about why she had decided, after all these years, to talk with her daughter directly about her childhood, what she hoped would come of it, whether she was really prepared. She called me the same evening to say she had remembered, from several years earlier, my offer to meet with them both and had, on and off, very seriously, been thinking about it. She felt that now the time was right, she didn't know why. Maybe it was one of those points where, if you didn't do something, their relationship might just blow up in one of their "horrendous" confrontations. Horrendous was a word her daughter also used to describe the fights between them, which arose, apparently over nothing at all, led to calls and letters, month-long silences, followed by a flurry of accusations and recriminations and apologies, which both women seemed to know had little to do with their contemporary relationship. Before she hung up, she said, "I don't mind if you take Stacey's side. I would expect you to. I'm just hoping, with you there, I'll be able to say something that might make a difference."

I wait for her to go on, she waits for me to say something.

144

"Well, I'm a mother too, and a daughter," I say finally, wondering how I will manage to hold both these women when we meet together.

"Yes," she responds, apparently reassured, "it's funny how you can be both at the same time."

They are both standing when I go to fetch them from the waiting room. Stacey springs forward to grab my hand. "Wow, hey, your hair is completely silver. Was it like that before? This is Mom. And we're both in green, wouldn't you know it?"

Mom smiles sheepishly, then brushes shyly at her skirt, as if she were to blame for the coincidence. "I didn't know what she'd be wearing. I haven't seen her, have I, for over a year?"

"Was I accusing you?" Stacey demands as they walk into the room. "Will you look at that," she says, in her self-proclaiming, vehement voice, "you've changed everything around. Okay, that's your chair? I'll take this one, I guess Mom can sit over there."

Mom seems pleased to have been offered a place. I feel relieved that Stacey hasn't taken my chair. Years ago, when she first came to see me, she demanded to know why I got the bigger, more comfortable chair. I answer questions like that and told her I needed a good chair because I was sitting for so much of the day. "Well, no one told you to do this work, I guess you wanted to," she responded, as if the only discourse she could imagine was a confrontational push and thrust. Later in our work she sometimes insisted that I had moved her chair further back because I was afraid to sit close to her.

"Chairs get moved around," I remembered agreeing, "put yours wherever you like, close or far is really up to you."

"But you did move it, didn't you?"

"Not that I'm aware of."

"Yeah, and I'm the only person with an unconscious in this place."

"Well, if I moved it unconsciously because I didn't want to be close to you, now I'm telling you consciously that we can sit as close as you like."

"That close?" she'd say, scooting the chair up to me. "That close?" she'd repeat, moving it closer, with a faint half-smile to acknowledge the provocation.

"Maybe you just want to forget the chair and sit in my lap?" I said one day when I was familiar with and somewhat tired of our little game.

"Maybe, maybe," she said, "just maybe," with a sharp, appraising glance, as if I'd finally said the right thing.

After that, the tone of our conversation changed, she became less challenging and belligerent, I became less apprehensive about saying the wrong things and setting her off, we settled in together and had some useful conversations.

She was twenty-eight years old at the time, a senior, a few months from graduation from UC Berkeley. She was a tall, lean, muscular woman, who walked ten miles a day while memorizing poetry. She wanted to be a poet and thought that if she filled her head with the best writing in the English language it would help her on her way. The poetry she showed me was tough, bitter and angry, with an incongruous, complex rhyme scheme and a wandering rhythmic structure. She had come to meet with me because she kept getting in fights with people at school, other students, her instructors, her adviser, a friend of mine, who had suggested she call me. It had taken her seven years to become a senior because of incompletes and unfinished assignments, although her grades, once she got them, were consistently good, and some professors found her writing outstanding. We had both been surprised when she was offered a place in a prestigious graduate program and discussed whether she should take it up or stay in Berkeley to go on with her work with me.

"Well, I'll go on," she had said, with a return to the belligerent mode, "if I can get my mother to come in with me. Why should I be doing all this work and she get off scot free? If she won't come, I'm off, we can forget this stuff and leave childhood where childhood belongs. In childhood."

"I'm not impressed with all this bargaining. You have your own work to do. What difference does it make if your mother wants to do it with you? It's your life. What you come to understand about it either matters to you, and helps you live it better, or it doesn't. What's that got to do with your mother and her choices?"

"I'm the crazy here, that's it? Is she spending three hours a week talking to someone about what a nut *she* is? The longer I stay here, the more proof she's got that I'm the one, not her."

"I thought you told me she feels guilty and uneasy about your childhood. Now you tell me she's trying to make out you're a nut? What's in it for her?"

"What's in it? You don't see? Who has to believe what a nut says about her childhood?"

"But who has ever disbelieved you? That's not the impression I got. You know and your mother knows what happened and that's never been an issue."

"See how you take her side? How do we know we both know if we never talk about it?"

"Oh, I take her side, and now you've got another good reason to stop our work together?"

147

"I thought you weren't supposed to get into arguments. I thought you were supposed to help me get on with my life. Okay, you decide. You tell me what to do. Should I stay with you or go to graduate school?"

"It won't work. You can't put that off on your mother and you can't put it off on me. What do you want?"

"I want out of here. You hear? Out of here. I've got a life. Why don't you get one?"

She had stood up next to her chair, glaring at me bitterly. Then she broke out laughing and sat down again. Almost immediately she jumped to her feet and began to pace back and forth in the small space between our chairs. "Okay. Okay. I'm going, okay? I'm going to graduate school. That's what I'm going to do. Okay, you listening? You're gonna hear this once, okay? And that's it. Okay, I'll miss you. That's it. It's over. Okay? I'm out of here."

And she was, after two more restless meetings in which we managed to clarify the reasons she felt it was so important to get her mother to come in with her. Stacey was determined to get her mother to face the question, "How could you?" She wanted her to share her point of view about the past and admit the errors she had made. She was convinced that their fights in the present could never stop until she got her mother to "face up to reality."

I thought "How could you?" sounded exclusively reproachful and was not a question likely to elicit information. Stacey vehemently disagreed. She wanted a "real" encounter, she wanted to speak her "truth." "How could you" was the only way she wanted to say it. A mother was supposed to protect her child. Stacey never had a mother! She had a dishrag, a wimp, who couldn't stand up for herself and couldn't stand up for Stacey. She was a disgrace to the name of Mother and Stacey wanted her to acknowledge that.

I thought that curiosity and interest were also part of Stacey's truth. What did her mother feel during those early years? What had she noticed about Stacey's suffering? How had she described it to herself? Wasn't Stacey curious about any of those things?

Those things, claimed Stacey, furiously, were exactly what she wanted to know, and even I would be able to see that if I didn't always try to apologize for her mother. She wanted her mother to admit the truth, that's all she wanted and she was damn well going to ask "How could you?"

I thought truth was not something people just knew; it emerged through dialogue or in the right kind of listening environment where risk could be taken and one could dare to face things one might otherwise avoid.

Stacey, raging at me: "You're trying to get me, *me,* to provide the right environment when it should be her job, that's a mother's job, she ought to be able to do something useful once in a while and so should you."

"I can help you with it, I can't make it happen by myself. Only you can get her in here and once here make it more or less likely for her to speak."

"You're just trying to get me to sacrifice myself to her and I'll be fucked if I'm going to do it. You hear? I won't fucking do it. . . ."

And now, here they were, years later, for a session during which I would have good reason to recall Stacey's furious refusal to sacrifice herself, take care of her mother or take responsibility for working things out between them.

Mother is an awkward woman, tall and strapping like her daughter, but reined in and apologetic, clearly a woman from another generation, as different from her daughter as mothers are likely to be, in spite of their similar short green skirts.

149

"So we're here," Stacey says, "what now?" Immediately, she is up and pacing, while her mother, looking scared, seems to scurry back into her chair.

I have an inclination, which I observe with interest, to put my arms around Mother's shoulders. She is a shy, timid, unassertive woman in her mid-forties who looks much older than her age. She works as an aid in a Catholic old people's home and is very proud of this job, which she has held for eighteen years. Stacey feels she is exploited and underpaid, Mother feels she "reaches" the old people, understands them and pays attention while the other nurses and aids just "do their duty by them." Whatever Mother did or didn't do when Stacey was a child, she's spent a lifetime in futile, feeble efforts trying to make up to her. She has cried, apologized, shouted when finally provoked, written tearful letters, left self-accusing phone messages, but has never actually spoken about the two years during which she and her seven-year-old daughter were living with a man—not the daughter's father—who was sexually abusing the child. Stacey, who has a highly developed capacity to rage and bluster and shout, has never been able to ask her mother anything about those years.

The two women could of course go on as they have always done, Stacey manufacturing a fight that lets them draw apart, often into complete silence for a time, after which they find their way back to one another. Someone in the family, usually Mother's sister, brings about a reconciliation, or Stacey comes back to California to stay with a friend and runs into Mother in the co-op. Tense, wary, suspicious of one another, the daughter because of the past, Mother because of the present, they find a stilted, superficial mode of engaging with each other until some small event sends Stacey into an uproar of reproach and recrimination, while

Mother, finally driven to exasperation, justifies herself with an un-characteristic and therefore always unexpected show of verbal force against whatever supposed harm she has just inflicted on her daughter, who refuses to forgive her until she acknowledges her fault, which Mother refuses to do, until the whole pattern repeats itself, as it might well do for the rest of their lives.

Now, the two women have agreed to meet together, with a lis-tener who has an interest in breaking open this pattern. None of us knows why this resolution to meet, avoided for so many years, has suddenly been taken. Perhaps Mother is ready to forgive her-self for what happened twenty years ago and can therefore tolerate Stacey's recriminations. Perhaps Stacey has asked in a less threat-ening way, making it seem possible that she really wants an answer to her question. *How could you,* still unspoken in this session, mutters restlessly through every silence, causing Stacey's belliger-ence, Mother's timidity and my sense of being on guard. If Stacey does what she has always promised to do with this confrontation, it might be better if we had not met at all.

So far, we have spelled out the basic rules of not interrupting until someone has signaled she has finished talking. Stacey has been pacing furiously between her chair and mine until Mother, who has been visibly shrinking in her chair, manages to say, in a faint voice, "I don't think I can talk until Stacey stops pacing."

"You see?" Stacey shouts, without looking at either one of us, "you see how she tries to control me?"

"Can you tell me," I ask, because I really want to know and I want Stacey to hear this response, "what it is about the pacing that makes you—"

"Go ahead," Stacey shouts, "take her side." She has come to stand next to my chair, hands on her hips, glaring at her mother, who straightens her shoulders and takes a huge breath of air, more like a gulp than a sigh, as if she were trying to breathe in a desperate courage.

"It scares me," she manages to say in an almost inaudible voice I somehow manage to catch, "the pacing scares me."

"What did she say?" Stacey demands of no one in particular.

"She said you frighten her."

"Oh shit," Stacey says, contemptuously, "I frighten *her*." Then she seems, very briefly, to consider this possibility. "Is that what she said?" she asks me, sitting down on the floor next to my chair. "Did you say that, Mom?" she asks, addressing her mother directly with the very slightest suggestion of some genuine interest. "I scare you?"

It seems clear that this possibility has never occurred to her. I realize that I should have told her, during our several months of work together, that I too was often scared by the unleashed force of her conviction that I had, through something I said, or a gesture I made, wounded her irreparably.

Mother, who is, I can see, sensitive to shifts of atmosphere and tone, takes heart from this one.

"Thank you for sitting down," she says, a comment that takes Stacey by surprise, as if she had not, before now, realized that she was sitting. When she starts to get up, I put a hand on her shoulder. She seems about to shrug it off, as yet one more controlling effort on my part, shivers slightly and settles into it, the nervous tension that has made her pace and shout visibly leaving her body through a series of quick muscular spasms and twitches I feel reflectively against my palm.

I glance at the clock. Fifteen minutes have gone by. Everyone seems exhausted in the sudden collapse of Stacey's tension. I decide to let the session go on until we reach some kind of natural stopping point, or someone just can't take any more, which could, I reflect, very well turn out to be me. Stacey would signal this end, if we are in the old pattern, by shouting and walking out. Mother, I can imagine, will lose her voice and fade back into the chair. I will be left feeling how tragically the pattern between these women proved, on this occasion, to be too much for us, and could not be broken. Perhaps another time? Maybe never? And that is where we are now, already face to face with this uncertainty, caught up in a silence in which, perhaps for the first time in their lives, this mother and daughter have a chance to strike out toward some new and different way of being together.

Mother's voice, when she begins talking, is still almost inaudible. Stacey, it seems to me, is about to comment on this. I press very firmly on her shoulder. She gives me a quick, belligerent look and again settles into the pressure of my hand, apparently relieved that I am containing her—a feeling that probably surprises her.

It is possible, even with a strained attention, to catch only a word or two of what Mother is saying. I hear, "state of mind" or "static," or perhaps "station" or "never mind," or maybe even "minefield." I have the impression she is repeating something she may have said so many times over the years, practicing up for an imagined confrontation, that she is now uncertain whether or not she is speaking the words out loud.

Stacey says, audibly, but very, very softly, "muttering to herself . . . that's what she used to be like . . ."

Mother, who has heard this, now looks up with a pathetic eagerness. "Yes," she says, seemingly relieved and surprised that Stacey remembers, "I was like that."

"She was," Stacey confirms, and the two women look at each

other, both somewhat shocked, across a shared recognition. Is this, I wonder, the first time they have agreed about anything in twenty years?

Things seem to be moving along under an internal impetus I am reluctant to interrupt. The two women seem comforted by the presence of a third person, who isn't required to do much except be there, holding things and bearing witness. I am, however, aware of the incredible ease with which everything could revert to an old pattern. Stacey could suddenly take offense, mother could apologize excessively, the fragile accord could so easily shatter. How to hold it? How to move it forward?

I am aware that Stacey and I, sitting together, across from mother, might seem to be ganged up on her. "Why don't we all sit down on the floor," I say, in the grip of a sudden, perhaps worthless, inspiration. Stacey shrugs (another controlling move on my part?), Mother looks startled. I slip down off my chair while Stacey, to my surprise, scuttles over toward me, as Mother, gingerly, perhaps aware of being on trial, settles herself closer to us in a small circle, a space somewhat less austere and formal, the companionable space, hopefully, of the campfire or a powwow.

Stacey, her bent leg almost touching her mother, unexpectedly leans over and pats her on the knee. Mother responds with a quick grab at Stacey's hand, which has slipped away, but not, I see, all the way back to Stacey. It remains somewhat indecisively on the floor between them, the palm open, the fingers twitching slightly.

It now seems clear that the three of us are in this together, and have, for the time being, broken out into a fresher air. Mother is staring at Stacey's palm, which has, perhaps, a look of invitation. Relieved to be here, I take a deep, audible breath, which Stacey imitates noisily, so that now Mother too, as if this were a code or a game, familiar to Stacey and me, joins in with us. Then, we all take a deep breath again while Stacey emits a vaguely friendly, childlike snort of laughter.

"Okay, Stace," I say, "tell your mother what you'd like to know."

Stacey is ready. She doesn't blurt or shout or evade the moment. "Mom," she says, very carefully, "I want you to tell me . . . and you know that's why we're here with Kim . . . so I want you to tell me . . . how could you . . . I mean, what was going on for you, you know, when Jimmy Kaye lived with us, and he was . . . and you knew that he was . . . you know . . . doing things . . . Mom, he was doing those things to me."

Mother, who may never have sat cross-legged on the floor since her own childhood, seems momentarily disconcerted by Stacey's directness. She begins to shift and move about, crossing and refolding her legs. Eventually she settles, clears her throat, makes up her mind to say something, hesitates and finally says, "I knew."

Stacey, who has always known that her mother knew, who nevertheless has been waiting twenty years to hear these words, receives them as if they were new, arresting and confessional. All remaining tension seems thoroughly to desert her body, which sags toward the center, shoulders curved, head thrust forward, with an odd grunting breath. She now offers, it would seem, no resistance to the older woman who can, therefore, finally speak.

But something instantly, I fear, is going wrong. ". . . sixteen years old . . . parents dead . . . taken in by Uncle Theodore . . . his son, Cousin Jason . . . got pregnant . . . Jason told Uncle it was someone else . . . Uncle didn't believe him . . . made him marry ... threatened, tricked him, disowned him ... never, he said that ... never see us again. Little Stacey, four years old ... Jason left us."

Mother is, if anything, overprepared for this moment; she has, inwardly, it seems, gone over these remarks, editing and revising them so many times, they now emerge with a trancelike irrelevance. She looks down blankly at her hands, meticulously folded or perhaps even clenched on her left thigh.

Stacey, of course, knows these facts thoroughly and has told them to me. She hasn't stirred or looked up once since Mother started talking. I can't read or even imagine her response to this fragmented droning. And now, because my own anguish over this situation gets the best of me, I say something when I would prefer to remain silent and let the two women work their way through this. I appeal to Stacey to keep going, to stay with us. "Mother wants you to know what an impossible situation she was in when Jimmy Kaye came along and offered to take care of you both ..."

Stacey lifts her head to look at me curiously. "I know what Mother is telling me," she says pointedly, as if it has just occurred to her that she has to protect her mother against my interference. "Just let her be," she adds, shaking her head; she seems to have known for a long time that I have trouble getting things like this right.

Mother glances nervously at me to make sure I'm okay. The protective gesture is not lost on her. If there were threads here tying the three of us together, those between Stacey and Mother have just been drawn tighter, while I have been slackened off. This is progress and now Mother takes heart.

The words that emerge now have a raw edge to them and she tries them out gingerly, as if afraid they could cut her. "I told myself we'd both die if Jimmy Kaye left us. So what he was doing to you had to be better than that. That's what I told myself, and I believed it."

A tense, anguished silence follows these words, which is finally broken by a tiny, childhood voice. Stacey says, "I believe you, Mom."

Has this really happened? Stacey, faced with her mother's spoken confession, has instantaneously passed beyond recrimination and reproach. She is soothing and sheltering the older woman. Is this what she was like as a child, before she was betrayed and abandoned?

Mother's delivery gathers force. "I told myself you didn't really know what was happening. You were asleep, or you were only a child, you wouldn't understand, you'd never remember. That's what I told myself . . . I told myself that . . . and I believed it."

"I know you did, Mom," Stacey repeats, in the very moment she might have cried out, "How could you?" Here is a Stacey, eager, conciliatory, protective, I had not yet glimpsed and had never imagined. A child-Stacey filled with anxious concern about a mother who must have seemed to her always on the edge of going under. Perhaps a hidden reason she brought her mother in here was to help take from the older woman her lifelong burden of guilt and self-reproach?

"No, it's not true, I never, I never once believed it," Mother cries out, while Stacey, very quietly, covers her face with her hands. "I couldn't believe it, I never managed to believe it, but that's what I told myself."

The anguish in these words has an immediate effect on Stacey, who stands up suddenly, lifts her arms and slaps them down against her thighs. She looks uncertain whether to shout or crumble and finally says, turning to me, not to her mother, "I can't take any more . . . I never could stand it when she was so sad. . . ."

I hold out my hand to her. She grabs it. "Even he, that fucking pig," she says, in an effort to get back into the anger that is now deserting her, "was fucking better than that." She points furiously at her mother, but I can see it won't work. Grief has caught up with Stacey.

Suddenly, I am imagining a child who knows things no child should ever know, a child who has seen into her mother's despair and therefore hands herself over to a grown man's grim hunger and lust to keep these off her mother. These are not ideas I have had before. Are they Stacey's?

I feel sure that any moment now a child is going to be crying. Stacey has come so close to this I myself can feel the pending eruption of a long-withheld sobbing. Stacey looks and feels to me like a woman at the edge of a momentous emotional discovery that will bring back into the present the lost years and abandoned emotional positions of her childhood. But Stacey does not cry. Once again she takes me completely by surprise, sits down quietly next to her mother, puts her hand on her mother's knee and says, "Okay, I'm listening."

Mother, as if unaware of an interruption, starts talking, quietly, fluently, and this time, finally, directly to her daughter.

"I listened," she says, as if she can't believe what she is saying, "I couldn't help listening, I told myself I wasn't listening, but I heard him. I can't explain it. Not now. Hearing, telling myself I was not hearing, convincing myself I heard nothing and still hearing. I saw how you looked in the morning honey and I told myself I saw nothing."

"Honey," Stacey says in a bland voice.

"I knew you were having a rough time at school and I knew why. Falling asleep in class . . . couldn't concentrate . . . bright kid like you. But I didn't let myself know . . . know and not know . . . not let myself . . . try not to . . . how can I explain it," she says, turning to me. "Can't you tell her?"

"That's okay, Mom," Stacey says, "I get it."

It is, by now, probably clear to all three of us that Mother cannot say anything Stacey does not know, nothing new to Stacey, nothing not already known to her in childhood. What Mother is saying is shocking and new only to herself, it takes her roughly out past the repetitive explanations she had imagined for this encounter through the long, silent years of preparation for this moment.

Stacey has been waiting twenty years to hear her mother speak these words. The need to hear them spoken directly to her, alive and happening in the moment, is so great it overcomes, it seems, every other possibility of feeling and reaction.

"I tried to blame it on you. I even tried that. I told myself it was you trying to come between us, as if you were jealous now that Jimmy Kaye had come to live with me."

"Yeah, Mom," Stacey says, clenching her fist. Something almost unthinkable is perhaps now being confirmed.

"I started to hate you," Mother says, staring at Stacey as if she were trying to make herself believe her daughter is here in the room and all this is really happening. "I hated you because he wanted you . . . and not me. . . ."

"Yeah," Stacey says tonelessly, and then in a grimmer voice, "I guess it worked."

Does Stacey mean what I think she means? Mother has no doubt about it. The words stop her dead. "Oh honey," she says, "oh honey."

We all wait. The clock, well-behaved until now, ticks and bangs incessantly. I hear the house creak and settle. Stacey shoots me a quick glare, cautioning me, perhaps, not to interrupt this.

"Oh, oh," mother gasps, "that's it, that's the worst of it. I knew you were doing it for me and I let you do it . . . I let you go in my place and I was relieved it was you and not me he did it to."

Mother covers her mouth with both her hands. Her eyes, terrified, startled, shoot anxiously back and forth between Stacey and me. Stacey sits rigid and still, meeting her mother's gaze. People rarely get what they have been waiting a lifetime to hear. On the rare occasions this happens, it is not the wish for revenge that gets satisfied, but something deeper and more archaic, as happens now, I imagine, to Stacey. The full meaning of her childhood sacrifice has just been recognized.

"Hey, Mom," Stacey says, coming very close to her, "let's not forget you threw the fucker out of there."

She did? Mother made Jimmy Kaye leave? This mother, who was sure they would both die if he left them? Had Stacey known this all along? Was she making it up or in the pressure of the moment, suddenly remembering?

Mother manages a grim, reluctant smirk. "But how in the world I did," she says, as if summoning the power to protect her child still seems beyond her, somewhat uncanny, not at all her own capacity, ". . . how in the world I did. . . . Still," she says, looking over at me with a bewildered acknowledgment, "Stacey's right. I threw the fucker out of there."

Was there something I overlooked, a hint, a clue I did not pick up, which might have prepared me for this revelation? The way, over the years, whenever Stacey pushed her far enough, Mother's temper flared and she was able to defend herself? I have trouble taking it all in. This timid woman, who shrinks in her chair while her daughter paces, managed to stand up against a man who terrified her, who seemed to be her only life support? Mother is smiling at Stacey, with a proud, sad, puzzled expression. Yes, she managed to get rid of Jimmy Kaye and Stacey has no doubt that it was done for her sake.

It is time for laughter and laughter comes, Mother's rusty, Stacey's mannered and insistent. But it is, after all, laughter and ushers in its own brand of freshness and relief.

"Mom said *fucker*," Stacey explains to me, in case I don't know why the two women are laughing.

"Yeah, the fucker," Mom repeats, savoring the redemptive pleasure of naming something correctly.

There is nothing hidden here that has suddenly come to light, no forgotten memory reemerging, apparently both women have always known that Mother got rid of Jimmy Kaye, but the fact seemed to have no relevance for either one of them. The encounter lay there, unused, unable to actively enter or inform their lives. They were caught and held captive by an incomplete version of their past. Here, in this moment, where the neglected episodes of Stacey's sacrifice and Mother's courage emerge, a pattern is broken, the pieces of their past are shaken loose and are now free to be rearranged in a way that will allow both women to make something new of themselves, and of their life together.

Because Mother has granted Stacey the full meaning of her childhood sacrifice, Stacey has restored to her mother the protective role she had, in fact, played. Her mother's acknowledgment liberates Stacey from the need to hammer away at what she feels she deserves from her. She is freed now; she has set out to free her mother.

Has someone just given birth? Certainly, in this radically revised version of the story, a woman who imagined she had sacrificed her child to save herself has been told that as a mother she also found the power to protect and save her daughter. The revisionist story has found two new, if belated, heroines: a mother who acted on behalf of her child, a child who sacrificed herself to spare her mother. In this process of confrontation, recollection and reconstruction, Stacey likewise gives birth to herself as the protective mother who must save the older woman from a lifetime of self-reproach. This is an outcome none of us could have imagined or predicted, a twin-birth for mother and daughter, both of whom, in this singular moment, have passed beyond the need for blame or forgiveness into a new vision of their complex history.

The two women look at one another shyly, unsure of what to say now that something so unexpected has emerged. The laughter gives way to a nervous banter. "Hey, Mom, didn't know you had it in you, did you?" Mom sighs and shakes her head and looks imploringly at me and tries to join in the banter. "Sure didn't, sure didn't," she says, "guess you just never know."

Before our session ends, this rearrangement of roles and positions becomes evident. Stacey, who will be taking off again for school, asks me to go on seeing her mother, who will, she feels, need my help to "absorb and integrate" what has just happened. Mother, who says she would be pleased to go on working with me, nevertheless refuses, so that I can continue to be Stacey's "special person." Stacey argues with her, a note of her old belligerence in her voice, but Mother is not cowed or coerced by it. She will accept a referral and continue this work her daughter clearly needs her to undertake, perhaps so that she herself is freed from the necessity to worry about her or do it for her. Stacey seems annoyed that she cannot get her mother to do this work with me, but satisfied when Mother suggests they both come back to see me together the next time Stacey is in town, an arrangement in which both women concede something to the other, and both get something significant and desired in return.

Will this negotiated truce between them hold? We probably are all asking ourselves this as we say good-bye, exalted by our breakthrough into possibilities that did not exist even three hours ago.

For the next weeks, Stacey calls me to "make reports." She wants to know if all abused children have a "martyr complex," a desire to sacrifice themselves for someone's sake? Is that how they manage to survive the abuse? By finding in it "their own meaning? Something redemptive?"

I also leave messages, encouraging her to go on thinking in this shadowy territory, where so little is understood. As the weeks pass, Stacey tells me that her personality has "come apart at the seams." She feels like a snake that has "lost its skin." She finds that "everything hurts." This, however, is tolerable, she says, because she feels "something growing." She's worried about her mother, a nagging, probably chronic concern she "kept out," she says, by being angry at her. She's not sure which feels worse, the anger or the grief and pity, but has decided to "go for" the grief because it feels more real.

I myself call Mother to check in with her and encourage her to follow through on my referral.

"I promised Stacey, so I'll do it," she says, "but I'm not sure what will come of it. For some people, you know, it might be better not to remember some things."

"Well, memory also holds some gratifying surprises, as we've seen." I'm afraid she may already have begun to discount what we discovered.

"I have to do it," she goes on, following her own line of thought, "to keep Stacey from worrying about me. That's what I have to do for her and I'll do it, but I'm not so sure it's for myself. . . ."

I wait, saying nothing, because I am thinking about this possibility.

"When you think," she says, "of that little girl sacrificing herself for me . . . well, I guess it's my turn."

"I have the impression you were not as impressed as I was by the way you managed to protect her. I hoped, in this work you might undertake, you would be able to discover the sources of precisely this kind of power in you and be able to draw on it. After all, Jimmy Kaye . . ."

"Yes, yes," she says hurriedly, as if to assure me our work has been good for her too. "I remember. Sure I do." Then, with her rusted laugh, she repeats the naming that has been, in her life, so late in coming. "Well," she says, "I know what I did. After all, just like Stacey says, he really was, you know, Jimmy Kaye the fucker."

PART III

A Wedding

٭

CHAPTER

12

.

$\mathcal{T}$o tell this story I must go back in time. These are college days during the late fifties. Back then, while I, in black stockings and turtleneck sweaters, was chasing after mind-expanding drugs, boys and "experience," Barbara was a founding member of Slate, the first political organization to emerge from the fifties ban on campus political activity. She was one of the first elected members to the student council, she ran on a political program rather than on "personality," and was successful in pushing through the students' right to advocate political action on campus. We were un-likely friends, of the kind that are deeply attracted to one another because of their difference and because they live in the same dorm. Even then, in our late teens, when I always seemed to my-self to be flying apart and heading off in a thousand directions, she had the ability to make me feel organized and composed, held together by the binding threads of her own strong personality, as if I had been tied into a precarious identity by the force of her sheer presence. I had once, as a student observer, seen her bring an unruly student council to order simply by getting to her feet, standing quietly until the uproar died down and then addressing her audience in a subdued voice with an unexpected carrying power.

In her graduate days she had gone to study in Berlin on a

Fulbright, married an older man, a member of the Kennedy administration, and moved to Washington, where she studied law and began her own career as a constitutional lawyer. Until the development of e-mail, our friendship had become a matter, over the years, of monthly and then not so monthly letters, all-night conversations in restaurants, during business trips.

I heard from her, shortly after her fortieth birthday, when she had been appointed to a highly responsible position in an international organization. She held the leading executive position in a humanitarian organization responsible for placing refugees from war-torn countries. She had been selected for the post for quite remarkable qualities of political savvy, prodigious organizational skills and a sense of humor that could survive late into the night under the most demanding circumstances.

Old friends meeting again after an absence tend to enact old patterns. I had invited her to lunch during the single day she was stopping in the Bay Area. That morning I had called her in Chicago, just before she left her hotel, to cancel our date because of a last-minute emergency with a client. She shrugged off the cancellation, took the matter in hand, although she would be returning to Washington the next morning. While I was closed in my study, working out the next steps for a battered woman who had just left her husband, Barbara arrived at my house, prepared a simple lunch for us from food she had picked up on the way, set the table on the deck and was pouring a glass of iced tea when I came out to greet her. She looked the way you always expected her to look, understated and elegant, in a simple, off-white suit with an almost imperceptible design in beige thread at the corner of the lapel. It expressed, as did all her clothes, even when she had been dressed in ironed jeans and a cashmere sweater, an aloof, almost regal coolness, which had always hidden, so strangely and evocatively, for anyone who knew her well, the deep sympathies, long-tested loyalty and passionate nature of my oldest friend.

She looked up to smile at me as I came racing out to throw my arms around her, feeling, as I always did when I first set eyes on her, the tense, visceral shock of our temperamental difference. She asked probing, attentive questions about my work with mothers and daughters. I told her that my daughter had recently moved back to the East Bay, after twelve years in Cambridge and four in San Francisco. I felt that she had come home and that I, after years of being "widowed" by my only child, had become a mother again. She raised her eyebrows at the word "widowed," considered whether it had been intended ironically, seemed to decide that it had been and turned on me a slow, acknowledging smile. Then she told me how she and Meera, the name her daughter had taken when she joined the monastery, had been slowly and painfully, over the years, making a relationship together.

Berkeley is having one of its rare summers without fog. Barbara says she has heard it is the most beautiful summer anyone has seen in Berkeley since 1958. We are reminiscing about how we used to study on the lawns without shoes or socks, a privilege enjoyed by girls who lived, as we did, in the co-ops but had been severely withheld from our upper-class sorority sisters. Suddenly, she tells me how deeply regretful she had been that I was unable to attend her daughter's wedding. "It struck me as odd," she said, in that subdued voice, "that you did not decide to come. It seemed, somehow, part of our friendship that you would be there and do everything in your power to get there, because that is the sort of thing you and I have always done."

It is a statement that contains no reproach and does not expect a direct answer. "I wanted you there . . . how shall I express it? For a key observer, yes, as a witness. It was the sort of event you would read so well and have helped me to understand better perhaps than I can without you."

"Not what you might have expected, or yourself planned, for your daughter's wedding?"

"You say that . . . because?"

"I've heard you talk about your daughter since she was a child. It has always been part of her nature to put her mother through severe trials. Wasn't it you who first told me that?"

"Trials her mother never passes . . ."

"And that, I take it, is the story of the wedding?"

"Story? Is there a story?"

"Always . . ."

"You imagine I am troubled by something I am not telling you about the wedding? But you are wrong, I assure you. It was, to begin with, somewhat chaotic, I admit. But it worked out beautifully by the end."

"So, end of story."

"You sound skeptical."

"Between 'somewhat chaotic' as a beginning and 'worked out beautifully' as an end, there has got to be a story. I'm listening, if you care to tell it."

"I wouldn't know where to begin."

"Let's see. You and Sam arrive in New York. You are staying, for reasons of economy I never understand, at the uptown office of a friend of Sam's, who is a therapist. It is . . . what? A hot and muggy day in mid-August . . ."

"There you reveal no prescience at all, simply your undying

grudge against New York because you weren't allowed to grow up there. But, in fact, it was hot and muggy."

If she were someone else I would jump up and hug her. Instead, I lightly touch her hand. "Let me give you a lecture. You've spent the last ten years rebuilding a relationship with a child who went far away from you at the age of eighteen. She's not the sort of person who offers explanations for what she's done and you are much too circumspect to intrude. So you've built up, very carefully, very cautiously, a somewhat fragile new life together. You've cultivated interests you have in common, you've given help whenever asked, tried not to offer advice, because it has always been resented and rejected. You and I, as friends, as mothers together, have spent the years since Meera came back speculating about why she left, but we don't know and probably we never will, because she will not tell us. We've had the impression she's been through a lot, more than she will ever admit to, perhaps. She has the look of someone who has suffered and brought herself back and returned to you as soon as she felt you could be proud of her. . . ."

"You are implying that her taking off, I mean, when she was a kid, had to do with a feeling that she could not live up to us?"

"You and Sam are a formidable pair."

Barbara picks up a straw hat put together from ribbons and paper flowers and bows. They were the wrapping for a present my daughter once gave me. It's an incongruous sight, my demure friend decked out in a wrapping-paper hat. The wasps arrive, attracted by the bright colors.

"This wedding," she says, ignoring the wasps, "was perhaps an indication on Meera's part that she was ready to enter our far more conventional world. She organized the event and sometimes, it is true, I could feel that her ability to carry it off, to make it successful, was a statement to me about herself. Perhaps, even a gift to me, or a gesture intended as a profound reassurance that she is now doing well in life. . . ."

She interrupts herself to lean toward me, both arms on the table in front of her. "Do you see why I so much wanted you to be there? With you there, even if we had not been able to say a single word to one another, this is the kind of conversation we would have been having."

We go into the kitchen for olives and goat cheese, she opens a bottle of old burgundy, the last of a vintage I found on a trip to the Napa Valley. I sip from her glass, refuse one of my own; wine is something I offer to other people. She seems surprised that I would have a wine this good and she is right. I bought it because it was getting old and didn't cost much, a wine-tale she seems to think typical of me.

There is a small window seat in a corner of the kitchen. We wind up here, side by side, instead of across from one another at the table.

"I was never asked to organize this wedding," she says hesitantly. "And I was never really even asked to pay for it. But I wanted Meera to understand that we would pay for a reasonably priced wedding of a sort she wanted. She already had a place in mind. Her fiancé, Jai, had been to some sort of show or concert there. Or maybe he had given one. He's a musician, in a category of music they call 'world music,' in his case with a very Indian influence. But it is electric music too, and certainly not what we would think of as folk music. The place they chose was part of the whole general plan. It was atmospheric, it wouldn't cost much, it had a great setting, or so I was told. It was represented to me as a boat, as a light ship, that had been scuttled off the Atlantic in the late forties and had been recently dredged up, and hauled and tied up to Pier 62 on the Hudson."

I try out the smile I reserve only for her. "How did all this sound to you?"

"It sounded like nothing to me. I mean, it didn't really bring up any image at all. As far as I was concerned, it might have been some enormous ship, like a ferryboat. Or it could have been something really quite small, like a yacht, or a tugboat, or those cruise ships that carry people around the bay for dinner events. It really brought up nothing at all. And so I didn't know whether or not this was an appropriate place to have a wedding. I just knew that it was a cheap space of some kind, where they wanted to get married. I have met Jai and I like him. He's been good for Meera, and she for him. And for them, somehow, the actual price of the place—which I think was about a hundred and fifty dollars—was so wonderful that it must have seemed as if the wedding was going to cost nothing at all, because they're just kids and their idea was that the rental of the place would be what was really expensive.

"Although, it's amazing that Meera, who has started her own small Indian restaurant in the East Village, could have thought that. In any case, I accepted it as a good faith effort at economy."

"Was she planning to cater it herself, perhaps?"

"I think 'planning' might be too active a verb. I think she had vaguely conceived that people would come to this ship and that there would be a ceremony of some sort, and then they would eat food that was provided by her, basically.

"At some point she said to me, 'Well, I've been talking to some caterers and they're all too expensive, so I think I could just make some tandoori fish . . .'

"I put my foot down at that point. I felt that it was risky to intervene but I said, 'No, you can't. You cannot make the food for your own wedding. You don't understand. That's not a possibility. It's too much work, you'll have a lot of things on your mind and a lot to take care of and it's just not possible.'

"She was planning to invite about a hundred people. Sam has a large family and so do I. Over the years she's become a very elaborate cook and she loves to give parties and she loves to cook for people, which is why she started the restaurant. So it took some convincing. I think she was imagining that part of the wedding would be a display of her culinary skills. So, I convinced her that she actually had to hire a real caterer, and the caterer would have to be in charge of everything, including the cake, which she also wanted to do herself. We argued about this. She gave in about the caterer, and of course I insisted upon paying. She gave in about that. But she was holding out for the cake. It went step by step. It was becoming one of those trials you say Meera always set for me. How much would I interfere? How much would I try to influence her? How much would I approve of things I really just can't approve of because I don't understand them? So the last trial was the cake, the insistence that in fact she had to have the cake made her way and made by her. She had brought a recipe from India for a traditional wedding cake, but of course the ingredients, even for someone in her profession, would be extremely hard to get and especially in time. She also had the idea that the cake should be shaped like a traditional American wedding cake, but with Indian ingredients and decorated with symbols from Indian goddesses . . . something else in which she has become an expert and which I, of course, know nothing about. But the cake was also supposed to look like it went with the venue of the dredged-up ship, so it would have to be a layered cake, with sea-symbols and nets and goddesses and mermaids, I suppose, all over it.

"Well, Meera hadn't actually seen the boat when these plans were being made. Jai had told her about it. When she did see it she realized that the interior of the boat was too small and obscure. There were a lot of cramped rooms on the main deck, which looked down into a very large hold that goes all the way down to the bottom of the boat.

"You might have trouble picturing this. The hold is the whole bottom of the ship, but it's got all kinds of machinery in it and it is actually the place where they planned to have their concert and dance, with Jai's musicians, that night after the ceremony. It's a huge metal boat, and when you play a lot of noisy electronic music in it, it reverberates effectively. But, on the main deck, with all these little rooms, there wouldn't really be a place to set up chairs and have a ceremony. Even the hold would be a little bit too small. And the question of how everyone would get into the hold of this ship was also difficult, because you have to go up and down ladders. Meera realized that. But at first no one knew how to solve the problem, and I myself didn't know because I had never seen the place and couldn't imagine it. Or perhaps I should, more truthfully, say: I was trying very hard not to imagine it. If this was one of those trials I was supposed to pass, even if I did not know it was a trial . . . well . . . better imagine nothing.

"The ship, though, is attached to a large barge at Pier 62; the barge is perfectly flat and it was included in the price of the whole space, so Meera and Jai realized they could have the ceremony on the barge, and then there could be a cocktail party, which would

175

be partly on the barge and partly on the boat, with people going back and forth between. There'd be a bar set up for each place, people could wander around, there'd be tables on the deck of the boat and tables on the deck of the barge.

"I was sent the menu, and I was asked to make suggestions on appropriate foods, which I did. But I could already see that this was a difficult position to be in. My suggestions might have seemed to reflect me and my values more than Meera's and her friends', but if I suggested nothing I would seem indifferent. I didn't want to suggest that the caterers prepare Indian food, which had been the original idea, because this would put them into competition with Meera. Jai's side of the family suggested a pasta buffet, Sam suggested poached salmon, which seemed a good solution to Meera and Jai, but I said no. I couldn't see a poached salmon buffet, with potatoes on the one side, and meat and pasta on the other side. Here, of course, I made my first of many slips because when Meera doesn't like a suggestion it feels like interference, which, in fact, on this occasion, I think I would have to say, it was. Over the years I have found that it is best, when she is preparing a meal, not to go into the kitchen. If anything is going wrong, she will blame me for it. It's the fault of my kitchen, or my knives, or generally my stupidity or my karma. She was like this when she was a little girl and is still like this, to some extent, since she has come back from India.

"Meanwhile, the cost of the event was growing. I mean, the wedding was clearly not going to cost a hundred fifty dollars, as Meera first imagined. That was hardly surprising to me. The week we got back from the wedding, there was a piece in *The New York Times* about weddings and it said that caterers—the top-notch caterers—consider a one-hundred-thousand-dollar catering bill to be moderate. And some of them refuse to do a wedding for that amount. They weren't talking about society weddings, but just upper-middle-class weddings. So, I was estimating at least—even though this was not to be a sit-down dinner—I was estimating that it would cost at least a hundred dollars a person. I thought that it would cost about ten thousand dollars. That didn't include the music, because there were musicians in addition to Jai's band. It didn't include the flowers, so I asked Meera what she was going to do about flowers.

"Meera and Jai were trying really very hard to keep the costs down, they were very responsible about this. They asked their friends and their family members to give them, as wedding presents, things that were actually part of the wedding, like the flowers or Jai's musicians. Meera's friend Ashanta was buying the flowers wholesale, and another friend would both be arriving from London the day before the wedding to do all the bouquets the day of the wedding, which was scheduled for six o'clock.

"Some of this was beginning to worry me because I realized that someone was going to have to be responsible for all these details and that Meera, who is not marvelous at organization, would already have her hands full getting married. So the dilemma arose again. Should I say something or not? Should I intervene or not? Should I offer help? These really are tests, aren't they? I would have organized things by just getting a lot more professional help. I would have gone to a florist and said, 'Look, this is a wedding, this is the location, this is the budget. What can you do for me?' But Meera went herself to a wholesale flower seller.

"Of course, I do not realize that all this is, to some extent, a test of my ability to let Meera do things her own way. But I sense the delicate ground we are on every time the telephone rings.

177

Remember, I almost lost this girl once, and for reasons I still do not understand. I can see that there is more than a wedding at stake here. But I can also see the whole thing blowing up at the last minute, and *that*, needless to say, is not going to be helpful either to Meera or our relationship. I talked all this over with Sam, and we decided to let Meera do things her own way. A few days before the wedding, she suddenly realizes that the flowers have to be put into something. Not only do they have to be picked up and brought somewhere and then brought to the boat and then arranged, they also have to be arranged in something, and by now we are getting very close to the wedding day. . . ."

Across the bay, the city is taking on mist. Over here, our day is still clear and bright, a small breeze coming down from a blue sky. The squirrel who has been eating our plants races across the deck. I listen for the muffled sadness evening brings in, but her presence keeps it off.

She takes my arm as we walk back onto the deck. "It is an odd experience," she says, "telling a story to you. To begin with, there seems to be no story. Then, the story begins to take shape and pretty soon I seem to know what you are thinking about it, even when you don't say a word."

"What am I thinking?"

"You've imagined this whole event, which seems to be a wedding, as a great drama between mother and daughter. Meera is marrying Jai, but a wedding of some sort is also going on between Meera and Barbara. In this case, there is no question that the groom will be standing at the altar, whatever that is, when the time comes. But, will the bride's mother be there? Will the mother and daughter make it through? It's more than a test, more even than a rite of passage. The bride and the mother are passing through an ordeal which will determine the fate of their future relationship, and this, perhaps—these are your thoughts, remember—is what weddings are all really about."

There is that smile she reserves for me. "I haven't made this interpretation, I've attributed it to you. You in turn haven't made it, you've attributed it to the story. Maybe it is Nobody's interpretation?"

"I admit to some thoughts. Hidden away behind the conventional wedding plot is the never-ending story of mother and daughter."

"What hidden plot will we discover next? Shall I skip over the next couple of days? Do you really want all this detail?"

"Every possible detail. Who knows where the secret keys to meaning will lie buried?"

"I really am getting nervous, you know. Telling you the story is becoming almost as big an event as the wedding itself."

"I'm listening. . . ."

"We're in New York. We've arrived at their apartment for brunch. They live in the East Village. A little, tiny apartment. They'd done a lot of good work so we're looking around the apartment and admiring it, we were having lunch and it was all just fine. And then Meera said that she needed eight hundred dollars in cash to pay the musicians, the ones who weren't part of Jai's band. These were the musicians who would play during the cocktail party and the dinner, before and after the ceremony, and they had to have the money in cash, they could not be paid with a check, *don't ask me why.* So Sam sort of raised his eyebrows a little bit, and Meera got very, very angry. Furious is the word. I didn't say anything about this, but I suggested that he go and talk to her about it. . . . What are you thinking? . . . I see that look on your face. . . . What just happened?"

"The whole thing could have blown up right there. This money question . . . every time it comes up the past is knocking at your door . . . whatever went wrong between you in the first place, Meera's running away to India . . ."

"Well, I asked him to go talk to her about it, and he did. She confesses that she feels unworthy of this whole event. . . . She was having trouble asking for money because she didn't feel she really deserved it. So, it was actually extremely difficult to reassure her that we had all along planned to pay for this wedding and didn't expect it to cost a hundred and fifty dollars. You are right about one thing: The whole wedding tested the old, old question of whether she could feel worthy enough to ask us to pay for this celebration. I suppose, in your dramatic version of events, if we, especially if I, had failed her here, or seemed to fail her, or hadn't been able to communicate that I was completely in support of this wedding, yes, she might, in some sense, have 'taken off to India again.'

"From the beginning, she didn't seem to be able to calculate what things were going to cost and ask for that amount of money. She seemed to think, Oh, well, I can certainly pay for the musicians, or I can certainly pay for the clothes for Jai's sons. And then she couldn't and would have to come and ask us for that money, and every time, yes, it's true, the old question of being worthy came up again. Back behind it all I began to sense how much shame and humiliation she felt each time. Every time the phone rang, for months, it was 'We'll need two hundred dollars for the man who's going to be officiating in the ceremony,' or 'We'll need two hundred dollars for the maid of honor's dress,' or whatever.

And the pattern continued right through the very day of the wedding itself. She just couldn't really bring herself to put it all together and figure it out in advance and I did not know how to help her with it. I just kept saying, every time she called, that I was happy to pay and had expected to pay. But she just didn't seem able to believe me. Why? You think you know why? What was happening?"

"A test has to be repeated. Suppose to begin with you had written her a check for ten thousand dollars? She'd have felt humiliated, she'd have swallowed her pride and she'd have accepted it. Or, she would have called the whole thing off because she didn't feel she was worth ten thousand dollars. But how you really felt, how much you were really behind her, she could only gauge by calling every other day with a request for money she felt she didn't deserve, until you reassured her."

"How do you pass a test you do not know your daughter has set? Maybe she was just unable to do it any other way. Organization is not Meera's outstanding characteristic."

"You can think of it like that."

"But you don't?"

"My analytic teacher used to say to me, 'Kim, not everything has a meaning.' But he could never convince me. A test doesn't have to be conscious, it could arise spontaneously out of the clash of personalities, the difference between two people, a mother and daughter in this case, who secretly long to be very much like one another, which, in this case, is impossible for them."

"You imply that every conversation between a mother and daughter, every plan, every invitation for advice, becomes a secret negotiation. 'Do you love me in spite of our difference? Will you put up with the way I live my life although it is so different from yours? If I press you really hard, will you still come through for me?' That really does go on between Meera and me. . . . But this time I stayed out of it and Sam went to talk with her.

"After the tears and the unhappiness at her apartment, which she recovered from pretty well, we took the subway uptown together, and she said, 'Oh, I've got so many things I need to do,' and I said, 'Well, why don't you tell me what they are and let me do some of them.' 'Well,' she said, 'I need to get lights for the tables that are going to be on the barge where we'll have dinner, because the caterers don't have any outdoor lights.' So I thought, Well, all right; that's interesting. The caterers don't have outdoor lights? But I didn't say anything. It turned out that the caterers could have done it, but this is what happened. Meera wanted the lights not to look like fancy dinner-table candle lights, but to look like lights that would be on an old dredged-up wreck. She wanted, you know, those colored glass candleholders with the plastic netting around them that used to be in all the seafood restaurants. That's what she wanted. So, she actually had gone around to places looking for these, because the kind of atmosphere she would provide was very important to her, but she hadn't been able to find any with the netting. So she thought she'd just get the colored glass ones and then she'd be able to make little netted socks for those. She's extremely handy and she can do anything she decides to do, but she can't do dozens of projects all at once two days before her wedding. That is what I couldn't get her to understand; that is where the difference between us really shows up, because I would not have driven myself crazy looking for these impossible details; I would have settled for less.

"By then she'd bought votive candleholders, but she doesn't want to use those. She wants to go to Crate & Barrel and get some sort of lanternlike things that she saw advertised in the paper. But of course, it is two days before the wedding, and she has a lot to do. A lot more in fact than I realized at the time. So, I promised I'd go and get these things from Crate & Barrel, and I did. Yes, I did. Sure, why not? What? What are you smiling about? Another test passed?"

"I'm just glad you didn't try to reason her out of what she wanted in the name of efficiency."

"And then there were the flowers. Well, she said, 'I have to go to the wholesale flower seller and make the list definite about exactly how many of which flowers I want.' I couldn't do that for her; she actually had to do that because she had very specific ideas in mind. But then I got very worried about what was going to happen to the flowers, because the wedding wasn't going to be until Sunday afternoon and it was now late on Friday and the flowers had to be picked up on Saturday. Where, I wondered, were the flowers going to stay over that night? I actually lost a whole night's sleep over this question. Well, I tried to give advice. I tried to say she should bring the flowers up to where we were staying, and she rightly resisted that. Although, the 'rightly' meant that her friend the flower-arranger, who would be staying in a hotel, had to have all of these flowers in her hotel room with her through Saturday night until Sunday, when she had to somehow get them all into a cab, these huge amounts of flowers, and get them to the boat to put them together into bouquets. I kept imagining what could go wrong, because Ashanta was arriving, remember, from London on Saturday morning. What if the plane was late? What if there was heavy traffic coming in from the airport? What if the wholesale flower place was closed by the time she got there? Things like that, which literally, kept me awake all night. I felt that I should do something, give advice, pick up the flowers myself, but something told me to leave it to Meera and her friend because I didn't want to give her the feeling that I had taken over and didn't think she could manage. Although I wasn't sure she could.

"I had not yet seen the boat, so on Saturday morning we went to see the site and have a rehearsal, and then have lunch. And first of all, of course, we couldn't find the boat. I thought we were supposed to bring the lights to the boat, so we were in the cab with all of these candleholders. And we get down to Chelsea Dock, which is where they say the boat is. We start asking people, 'Have you heard of a club called The Anvil? Do you know where it is?' And they say, 'All the clubs are out there,' and they point out to some very posh-looking ships, and so we think, Okay, that's where it is, somewhere there. So we start walking, with all these candleholders, and we walk and we walk and there's no ship called *The Anvil*. So we then come all the way back to Chelsea Dock and we notice Jai standing out in front of what looks like an old abandoned warehouse, with broken glass strewn everywhere, piles of ashes, just really something out of a Dickens novel about the Thames before the embankment was put up. And we say, 'Jai! Where is it?' and he says, 'Oh, it's in there!' So, we say, 'In where? There's nothing in there.' But, there is. That is the entrance to it; you have to go through the puddles and the piles of debris and all of this stuff, and you come out on this barge, which is, once you get there, just a great big . . . barge. You go along the side of the warehouse, and you come out onto a pier, and then onto a very large metal barge; which has all sorts of quite rusty structures and pipes and things lying about. And that's the barge, the wedding barge. What? You want me to tell you how I felt? I felt nothing. I was spending all my energy just taking it in. Well, maybe I felt something like . . . maybe it was . . . in any case, it was certainly something I, as a mother, wouldn't want to feel. . . . Do you know what I mean?"

"I was wrong. This isn't a test. It's a series of trials. A great hero's journey, set up for the mother, who has to show everything she's made of if she is to get through. Mythology is full of it."

"And if she gets through it? What then?"

"She still has the daughter. She will have been given away in marriage, but the mother will still have her."

"You understand, the barge is really just a big, flat projection out into the Hudson. It's metal on the bottom, but they've put down some spongelike tiles so people can walk on it without slipping around. And then it has these rusty structures, metal pillars overhung with a metal canopy. And one of those structures is actually like a little stage: It's up about two or three feet off of the ground. That stage, which is at the far end of the barge, is to be the place where the ceremony will take place.

"What did I think when I saw it? I thought that it looked like . . . an old, rusty barge. I had tried not to picture anything, but this wasn't what I hadn't pictured. First of all, you couldn't tell it was a barge. It looked sort of like . . . a pier. It just looked like a working pier. It had lots of coiled rope lying about, it was the sort of thing a tanker would pull up alongside and you'd start unloading it. That's what it was. It didn't look like a social venue of any sort. But it turned out that it was much better than the boat, the ship itself. Although quite wonderful-looking from the outside, when you got inside, the boat was really . . . it was just, just rust, and one little rusty room after another, more or less rusty ladders going up and down. There were toilets that were more or less useable. And then there were some rooms that were sort of furnished with junk, I mean, really junk, like from a Kienholz installation. All sorts of cobwebs and exploding upholstery and things like that. You just wouldn't want to put anything down in any of those places. But that's also where the bride and the bridesmaids were going to get dressed for the wedding, and wait for the event to happen.

"Well, it's about ninety degrees outside. Inside this completely metal structure it is of course about one hundred ten degrees. That's why it's called The Anvil. I mean, why else?

"The next afternoon, when we were actually preparing for the arrival of the guests, it became clear that a lot of the lightbulbs in this place were not exactly working. So, for example, the ladder-like stairs going down to the toilets were completely dark. And remember, this was just one big hole that you'd fall into. I mean, you really couldn't see anything coming in out of the semilight into this total darkness.

"But on my first view of the place, I wasn't taking in such details. I was still trying to envisage it. How is this wedding going to take place? I couldn't figure out what it was going to be like, but all the young people seemed perfectly happy. All of the bridesmaids, Meera's cousins, Jai's cousins, and her friends and all of Jai's friends and especially his little sons. Most of the ushers and his best man were from his band, and his brothers were there and they seemed very pleased with the place. They'd been there before for parties and theater shows and dances and stuff like that. So this was just part of what they thought of as a kind of cool place to be. Meera's interest in it I think is actually a little more of an interest in ships. I think she likes it as a kind of museum, a maritime museum, this place that was frozen in time. But I think also she likes unusual juxtapositions, a wedding, which is a traditional idea, in a place that is, to say the least, not at all traditional. I was thinking about it in this way because I couldn't otherwise make any sense of it. I mean, it did not look like an easy place to have a wedding, to me. If what we were looking for was convenience, this was not what we were getting. I could see that this place was completely inappropriate if what we're doing is trying to look normal. But we're not trying to look normal. And, it occurs to me, who should we try to look normal for? I kept saying to myself, This event is not for me, but it won't really shock any of our guests, either. My family is certainly not going to get freaked out over something like this. No, not even my mother. Because she's just seen too much. She has four children of her own and, well, we are what we are. I'm sure, she can't brag about this wedding, but I think she'll understand it. I was still nervous mainly because I thought that small things hadn't been done.

"So I said to Meera, 'Where's the dress?' And she said, 'It's still at the dressmaker's.' And I said, 'It's Saturday, and the dress is at the dress—' And she said, 'We're going to have lunch; we'll pick it up after lunch.' And I thought, Pick it up after lunch? Today we're having the rehearsal, then we're having lunch and then we're going to pick up the dress? What's going through your mind? This is what I was thinking. But I didn't say it. I said, 'Let's call the dressmaker and make sure she's going to be there.' 'Oh, she's always there,' said Meera. She lives in the East Village.' So I thought, Okay, if she's not there we'll get a mermaid costume. That will go with the nautical theme.

"So, we have our rehearsal, which was sort of chaotic, because nobody knew what to do. Meera had a book, and she was planning to do everything by the book. It was one of those books that tells you what the order of procession is, and things like that.

Only, everybody had different ideas, and none of us really thought the book was right. So we kept arranging and rearranging everything. We were deep in confusion by the end of this rehearsal about who would walk in what order, who would walk with whom, and what music would be played. In fact, I think we came away feeling more confused than we were when we started. All we had done was to plumb the depths of our ignorance about how this wedding should be done. This traditional wedding on a salvaged wreck rusting away on the Hudson."

We go down into the garden to pick some lettuce and a few small zucchini. The tomatoes are not yet ripe, snails have been snacking their way through the radishes. I've planted salvia to draw in butterflies, flapping low now in the near dark. I pick wild strawberries, the small, pointed, pungent kind you get in France. I fill her hands with them; we carry the lettuce back into the house.

Even if this takes all night, even if we talk until morning, even if we go out wandering through the Berkeley hills, our separation is already on its way. The wedding story will come to an end and we will be parting.

"Tell me about the lunch after the rehearsal," I say, to get her going again. "I have the feeling it was a lunch like no other."

"Yes, you're right. It isn't what you would call a normal lunch after a wedding rehearsal. It was the first time we were going to meet Jai's parents, in the East Village, just across the street from the dressmaker. So, for most of the lunch, Meera and I were jumping up and running across to the dressmaker, and running back. We were trying to find out if all the dresses were ready, and having final fittings so that if anything needed to be adjusted there would still be time to do it. The fitting and adjustments took place during the lunch, and they involved also the two bridesmaids, Meera's cousins, who were at the lunch and also had to go over and try on their dresses because they too hadn't picked up their dresses yet. Then there were Jai's twin sons from an earlier marriage, who were to be the ring bearers, wearing some sort of almost traditional Indian garb, which the dressmaker had made according to a pattern of Meera's. They are little boys, seven years old, very polite and well-behaved but not very patient with standing around being fitted. And so we were trying to organize people and clothes, and there was a big traffic back and forth across the street, into the restaurant, over to the table, up and out again and back to the dressmaker. Meanwhile, I found myself criticizing the dresses in little ways, which by that time I could not keep myself from doing. For example, there were still hooks and eyes that needed to be done, especially on the bridesmaids' dresses, and there were just lots of little things that looked to me as though they might need adjustment, but you can't tell because the dress is not really finished yet and in some cases not quite exactly ready to be tried on. Or, the dress is not ironed, so it's hard to tell how it will hang, and these dresses are pretty elaborate; there's a lot of material and they are fairly heavy dresses. So I was asking the seamstresses to take the dresses out and iron them and bring them back; and this sort of pressuring and managing went on all afternoon. But suddenly I asked, 'Where's the veil?' I'm calm. But I'm wondering, Where's the veil?

" 'Veil?' says the dressmaker. 'Oh, a veil? Did you want a veil?'

"Well, it's a hundred and I don't know how many degrees outside, and the little shop isn't even air-conditioned, so we're all standing on the stoop and fanning ourselves, sweating and swelling. And it's the middle of the East Village, you know? In the

189

East Village everyone's walking around with things like tongue-bolts and tattoos everywhere, piercings, these bizarre rubber suits that they wear in a hundred-and-twenty-degree weather . . . well, it's not the Waldorf; it's not an atmosphere that increases one's sangfroid. Meera seemed surprised that the dressmaker doesn't remember about the veil, because it had definitely been ordered. 'Oh, okay,' said the dressmaker, 'I can make a veil,' and she snaps her fingers, 'like this.' Okay, I thought, Make a veil *(snap, snap)*—like this. Of course, it took another hour and a half for the veil to get done, or two hours, or whatever. It was then late in the afternoon, and everyone had gone home and Sam and Meera and Jai and I and Meera's mentor, who has helped her with the restaurant, were sitting in the bar across the street, waiting for the veil to get done, and waiting for the dress to get ironed, and we were talking about how much cash we'd need for the next day. The musicians, Meera reminds us, have to be paid in cash. So Meera's mentor jumps up in a grand gesture and he says, 'Oh, I'll pay. I'll throw in two hundred bucks for the musicians. Just show me where there's an ATM machine.' So Meera and he get up, they go out in this very chummy fashion and they come back and, of course, he didn't have any money in his account.

"Meanwhile, all that day, every time Sam and I passed an ATM machine we'd stick in a card and take out two hundred dollars, just like that. Just every time. Two hundred dollars, two hundred dollars, two hundred dollars. We got about a thousand dollars on Saturday and by the next day, it was gone.

"Well, the dresses were finally done. Only then did I learn that I was not only to pay for the dresses, I was also to take them away and be in charge of them. It was my job, as the bride's mother, to get all these dresses from where I was, in the East Village, to uptown where we were staying, and then from uptown down to The Anvil, along with the other things, like the lanterns, I was to bring to the wedding celebration. We were still carrying these lanterns around with us because Meera didn't want to leave them at The Anvil overnight. So we had lanterns and dresses, thousands of dollars in cash, and by that time I was really glad we didn't have the flowers. I was still pretty calm at this point. I was fairly calm. I don't know why. I think I'd given up on it going smoothly. I was just sort of drifting with the tide of events. I'd entered a state Meera would probably very much approve of, and in fact we are getting along pretty well. Somehow, instead of dragging her into my anxieties, I'd gone over to her side of things.

"What? What is it now?" She interrupts herself. "There you go," she says to me, with one of those impish, tender expressions so rare in her they have become, for me, over the years, unforgettable. "Am I supposed to imagine that I've done something important, very highly significant in relation to my daughter by being able to enter her state of mind? To drift along and to let things happen?"

"It's not what you'd call, exactly, characteristic."

"You really are, you know, in spite of your silence, the most story-shaping listener I've ever met. I'll try to ignore you. I'll tell you the story; you make of it whatever you like."

She takes a deep breath and looks rather dazed, it seems to me, as if the story has got hold of her and will make her tell it to the end. She also seems tired, adrift in an unfamiliar dimension. Unexpected details keep swimming up, odd twists and turns to meanings emerge and there is, of course, my insistent presence. Should I bail her out? Should I suggest we take a break for a few hours? But she had already resumed the story.

"So that night before the wedding I was supposed to get all of my family—all thirty-two of us—to a little Italian restaurant back down in the East Village, contact them all to make sure they've arrived, let them know where the restaurant is, what time we're having dinner: seven o'clock that night. Well, I tell myself, that's time enough to get uptown with the dresses and the lanterns and make the calls and then start down to the East Village again. I am, remember, the mother who has no particular organizational role in this wedding, but it is clear by now that someone is needed to tie these threads together and that someone, I suppose, purely be default, is me. Meera had chosen the restaurant and made the reservations, and what I had initially planned, because that is what we do in my family, was a kind of no-host dinner in which my sisters and I would each of us pay for the members of our individual families. That's the way we had arranged it. So there were thirty-two of us, with step-children and divorced ex-husbands and sons-in-law and divorced ex-daughters-in-law, and we had taken over a really very large section of the restaurant. It was a good restaurant. It was delicious food, and it was one of those New York Italian restaurants with great noise and bustle—to which we contributed our share. We were a great big family, taking up one end of the restaurant. There was a little table for two close to us, and couples would come and sit down there, and they would leave within five minutes. They just couldn't stand us. And of course, people in our party were still arriving at seven forty-five, and the waiters were realizing we would be hard to get rid of. And then the ordering was chaotic because my brother-in-law Theodore had been told by Meera that he should order for everybody, so he did, but then other people didn't understand that, and they ordered for themselves. We had just plates and plates of food. We said to the waiters, 'Well, we're going to share all of these plates.' And the waiters said, 'Okay,' so they just put them all down in the middle of the table. Then it took a long time for the waiters to realize that we also had to have individual dinner plates that we could put the food on. It was one of those evenings when you actually had to get up and talk to the waiters constantly. 'If you would do it this way, I think we could manage. . . .' Of course, it was I who had to get up to talk to the waiters. After a few hours, Meera and Jai got quite tired, and they left. They knew the account was to be settled by me and my sisters. I went to the cashier and I said, 'Could you split this according to our family groups?' I had already added up the number of the people at the table, and the proportion belonging to each sister. We did it on a per-person basis, dividing the shares per family. I'd done all of the calculations. But when I asked the cashier, 'Can we split it on the cards this way?' he said, 'We don't take credit cards.'

"Meera had made a reservation for thirty-two people at a place that does not take credit cards. Well, thank God, I say to myself, for those thousands of dollars. But of course, having used them to pay the bill, we then had to walk all over New York the next day looking for ATM machines to take out more thousands of dollars.

"Now the wedding day—the wedding day— Oh, the wedding day. There were a number of little problems. For example, there was no hair dryer because we were staying in a friend's office. We were staying with a guy who is a divorce therapist, so everywhere strewn around this office were books like *Divorce Today* and *Divorce New York Style* and *How to End Your Marriage and Preserve Your Family*. I mean, everywhere you looked. It really was the most inappropriate place that people who had arrived in town for a wedding could possibly be staying. When we woke up, the morning of the wedding, our friend was using the office of his partner right next door. And there was a couple in there screaming at each other about how they were going to kill each other, on Sunday morning, the morning of our daughter's wedding. I do not read things as omens. I don't believe in them and I have no trouble convincing myself that it is really just incongruous that we are where we are and overhearing this murderous fight.

"Most of the setup for the wedding on the boat was being done by the young people. We knew we were not going to be much help with that. I was determined to bring the dresses at the last minute so that they wouldn't get ruined. The caterers would be bringing the food and the tables and the chairs. So, at that point, I figured that if anything really disastrous were going on, we'd be called about it.

"Sam and I start to leave about three in the afternoon, with the dresses and the lanterns, and just then, I mean just as we started to leave, it started to cloud over. Then it started to rain. And this was an outdoor wedding, remember, on the barge. Then, the thunder and lightning came. And it really, really came. Gale winds. And the tent that we had set up the day before—we of course didn't know this yet—but the tent we set up just in case it rained, had been lifted off the barge by the wind and dumped into the Hudson, where it went floating away.

"Meanwhile, we were waiting for the rain to die down. What else could we do? I may be the bride's mother and better at organization than she, but I could not stop the rain. When we finally arrived at The Anvil, people had huddled inside this rusty barge, and it was leaking like a sieve. There were just huge blotches of rusty water falling all over everything. The tables hadn't been put up yet, so that at least hadn't been ruined. The tent had been retrieved, but it was dripping wet, so it couldn't be put up again. And it was still very threatening—there were still very dark thunderclouds in the sky in every direction, so we really just did not know what was going to happen next. By the time we arrived there was a sort of cleanup going on, but in the cab I was just despairing. I finally gave in, I couldn't figure out what was going to happen, but I thought, Well, you know, we could all gather in that warehouse. We could have the ceremony in the warehouse, then we'll kind of dash into the boat. . . . I mean, I just couldn't imagine what we were going to do. I'd almost gone completely blank. I couldn't calculate what all the contingencies might be.

"But once we all got there everybody had something very specific to concentrate on and that seemed to help. It put the larger question of how this whole thing would be managed to the side. Meera concentrated on whether or not she could get into her dress without being seen by people who were arriving. All the different bridesmaids were in their own rusted dressing rooms, each concentrating on how to get dressed, stay clean and not be seen. Jai worried about whether or not the flood and the leaking of the boat had shorted out the electronic circuits that his band would need after the wedding ceremony for the dance that was going to take place in the hold. So he goes down below and plugs in the amplifier and . . . well, it explodes! It explodes and it catches on fire. And his mother says to me, 'It's amazing. Sometimes the musicians do that for show, they blow up their instruments, but right now there is nobody here to see it.' What is her tone? I wonder. What is the tone of all this? Ironic, very affectionate, and above all, accepting: 'Well, I know my son . . .'

"So now Jai, now the groom is, of course, leaving. Now Jai is leaving as we're coming, and he's in his shorts. He's shirtless and in his shorts. And he's leaving, because he has to get another amplifier. So I'm just getting blanker and blanker. I mean, weddings are sometimes late because the groom isn't there, right? You might even think of that as a somewhat eccentric part of a traditional wedding. We have managed to deal with the rain and the wet tent and the dripping rust and the threatening thunderclouds, and the explosion and the fire and the groom leaving in his shorts, so I am busily now trying to figure out how I could be useful, so I'm sort of looking around at things like whether there are lights over the stairs that go down to the toilets, things like that. I'm becoming interested in little things like that that might become dangerous. I'm trying at this point to stave off major injury. Okay, I've decided, I'm going to focus on potential injury for the guests because frankly this whole thing has got beyond me and I don't know what to do. So I keep looking around trying to figure out, what are the real disasters that could happen here? I'm going to try to get this place up to code. Which means finding the actual owner of The Anvil, as opposed to the caterers and people like that who have come in from the outside. Suddenly I'm absolutely determined to find him, to get him to do things, to get him to notice, for instance, that this light's out, that light's out and this place is slippery here, it might be safer if we moved these things out of the way and stored them in the back of some other place. That was the sort of conversation I wanted to have. Well, I found him. I found him. I think he was in the warehouse. Where else would the owner of The Anvil be? But then some of the musicians, who have begun to show up, don't want to play because they are afraid that their instruments are going to get wet or explode, or catch on fire, you know, absurd fears like that.

"What else? Oh, what else? So one of the ushers didn't show

up. I don't know why. I guess he got caught in the rain, so he probably thought the wedding was off and he didn't show up. We then had to designate another usher and explain to that usher what he should do and things like that. This was of course not easy because, ever since the rehearsal, we all knew that we didn't know what to do. So it was just one thing after another, just one difficulty after another, little tiny difficulties, one after the other.

"Now it is about six o'clock, and that's when the wedding was supposed to start. But people were late; people were late because of the rainstorm, so people didn't really arrive until between six-fifteen and six-thirty. Then another problem emerges. No one had put up the sign outside that I had suggested, saying where the place was, so that people would know, when they arrived at the warehouse, that this was the venue for the wedding. Or maybe the sign had blown away. That now was another thing we had to do, we had to put a sign outside telling people they had arrived, this place, this warehouse, this rusting barge on the Hudson was the site of the wedding.

"By this time Meera was very nervous. Whatever she learned in the monastery didn't seem to be much help now. And she was mainly just angry about the fact that people kept coming back to the part of the boat in which the bride, who should not be seen before the wedding, was getting dressed. In the midst of all this pandemonium she had decided to concentrate on that one terribly important detail of a traditional wedding. Finally, she decided she would have to go down and stand in the dark hold of the ship. The wet, dripping dank hold of the ship. So that's what she did. She went down, with some of the other girls, and stood down there holding her skirt up until the wedding was ready to begin.

"But what kind of wedding were we going to have? Everything, basically, that my daughter had planned and worked for with so much effort, to prove so much to me and to herself, was at that point in flux. All we could do was make the best of it and hope we could laugh at it someday. But maybe not. Maybe not . . .

"Suddenly things brighten; it is not raining; the chairs have been set up by the caterers on the barge, the food and tables are arranged and the procession, some sort of procession, is going to take place. The ushers and the bridesmaids processing down the 'aisle' together, because all along the guys have wanted to process down the aisle too. They are planning to come down in pairs and then split off and stand on either side of where the groom is standing. Jai has been planning to do the right thing. He has come back, taken care of the amplifiers, got himself dressed and goes directly to the altar, where he very appropriately waits for Meera. In the last minute, during the rehearsal, it was decided that his twin sons, the ring bearers, will not process. They will stand up with him and the three of them will wait for Meera. The audience is supposed to be sitting on the barge, facing the so-called stage where the ceremony will take place. I'm the mother of the bride, so I'm supposed to be the last person to be seated by the best man, just before the procession starts. I therefore am not supposed to be in the procession. My seating is the signal for the procession to begin, but during the rehearsal no one was ever able to get this right. The signal kept getting lost, maybe because a lot of Meera's friends didn't realize that I'm Meera's mother, and so my sitting down or standing up does not make much of an impression on them, or on the musicians, who are supposed to start playing, or on anyone else. We had gone over this many times during the rehearsal. But the best man wanted to come back and walk the maid of honor down the aisle, which is not normally done. My feeling during all this had been, I think it's best if people make up their own ceremonies. If this feels right to this group of young people, then this is what should be done. That was very, very clear to me. There were some standards, some rules by which they were all playing, and little by little they seemed to be working out something. I began to get the sense of something very authoritative in Meera, of her knowing how she wanted things done, and of making her way toward that and not needing really either my help or interference. And now, on the day of the wedding, after the storm and the rust and the dripping and the explosion and the fire and the late guests, I started to feel the same way again. Somehow, they will find the way to make their procession and have their wedding.

"And they did. The sky cleared, it cleared very dramatically, and this happened, really, just before the procession started. The thunderclouds disappeared just as people started sitting down. It was almost as if people didn't want to sit down unless they could tell they were not going to get rained on. And then the sky did clear. And it got extremely beautiful. From that moment, the evening became breathtakingly beautiful. Everyone's spirits lifted; there was a true sense of euphoria, the musicians arrived and they started playing and suddenly I could see that Meera had chosen the perfect setting. There we were on the Hudson, the river was glassy and reflecting pastels. There was the Statue of Liberty in the distance, and the Empire State Building on the Manhattan side. And the sky, the sky was really extraordinary, a very colorful sky, lots of grays and blues and pinks and greens. And then other boats started coming by, other weddings came floating by on boats that were actually afloat and moving. There were Jamaican Saturday Night parties going by, with lots of drums and people dancing on the deck and then of course I realized that she had been absolutely right, that this was just a splendid place and that one couldn't for any amount of money have found a more beautiful place in the entire island of Manhattan. No, and one certainly couldn't have found a place more like Meera, in the ways that matter. She is a woman who likes the idea of having a theme or a motif that she can work with. Getting married was perhaps an indication that whatever had been wrecked in her life has now been salvaged. But she doesn't want people to forget that she had been submerged. She doesn't want to be cleaned up and renovated and normalized. She doesn't want the conventional lovely wedding. She wants the exploded upholstery to show. She chose her theme, the salvaging of the wreck, and she made it into a fully appropriate marriage statement."

We have been sitting on the stairs that lead to the rooms on the second floor. She, taller, a little bit older, sits on the step above me. Outside, lights come on and go off according to some rhythm of their own and at last daylight shows up. The story has come to an end.

She is my oldest friend and she is leaving. She gathers up her things, refuses to let me drive her to the airport, calls a cab. We wait for it outside on the street. Early morning is wet, the dew is in her hair. "So," she says, returning to the easygoing tone that will allow us to say good-bye, "do we fit? Do we match up with your schema? Are Meera and I women who have given birth to our mothers?"

"I don't know. Not exactly. I wish you matched. It's always better for a storyteller when something conforms to a preestablished thematic pattern."

She detects a note of sadness in my voice, but it is not for the failure of my grand design. "Maybe we don't quite fit because in its strange, unconventional, but highly dedicated collaboration, Meera and I managed to create a new relationship and therefore no birth and no mother was needed."

"Couldn't we call that new relationship the mother to whom you both gave birth?"

"The trouble with this concept is its infinite flexibility. Anything can be made to be its illustration."

"Well . . . are you so sure Meera didn't make something new of you by forcing you to survive the wedding, as you did, without once, not once, letting her down or failing to support her? In my sense, yes, she did give birth to the mother she needed you to be. You passed all the tests, you survived the ordeals and the trials and you emerged, triumphantly, one could say, celebrating your daughter's vision."

"I have been listened to," she says with that air of subdued finality that has taken her so far in life. "I've become part of your story. If I choose, I can understand Meera and myself through it, or I can go back to my old way of thinking about us."

"Your old way?"

There is that smile she reserves only for me.

"That there really wasn't any story. It began chaotically, as I said, and it ended well."

"It ended well."

"It's very odd to be part of a story," she says reflectively as she hugs me good-bye. "It's as if I have given myself over to you, to compose and edit and interpret. I leave here a little less my own, a bit more yours. And why not? Why not, after all?"

201

To make up for what I have taken, I offer her the hat with paper flowers and bows. She chooses instead the plain straw hat and sets it somewhat rakishly on her head. "This much, at least, I agree we have learned," she says as she leans out of the car to kiss me good-bye. "No matter what you think you are doing in life, the mother is always there."

"Always the principal, if hidden, player, even when the daughter thinks she is spinning the event."

"I wouldn't go that far," she says as the cab carries her away.

What has to be said has been said: I, in the silence that follows, that finishes and completes a story, can only wonder what Meera will make of her wedding when she tells about it someday, perhaps to her own daughter. It could be that she, with her interest in folklore and mythology, will agree with me that she sent her mother through a great transformational ordeal, requiring her to do things in the daughter's way, to support but not to take over the enterprise, to hold it together for the daughter's sake and not for the sake of appearances, to join and engage in something she does not understand, to enter so far in that she touches, for a moment, her daughter's way of experiencing life.

But the wedding itself. Will Meera ever really be able to describe it to her daughter? Does she appreciate its haphazard peril, so full of her own demanding sense of beauty? Her need to pattern the significant events in life according to a grand theme? Her sense of ironic incongruity, which yokes together the conventional with the bizarre? Will she ever be able to describe the mysterious way in which the wedding held the tension between the traditional and the iconoclastic? Or how it held, to the very last moment, a highly individual sense of style? For it was style, style indeed, that created this eccentric wedding, in an idiom, it is true, very different from that of her mother—but a high style nonetheless, which bears the evident marks of their enduring kinship.

No, I suppose it would not be Meera who could describe her wedding. That task had been surrendered to the mother, as talebearer, as storyteller, for the culminating trial in her transformative ordeal.

EPILOGUE:
A STORY THAT HAS NO END

$\mathcal{T}$he three of us rarely spend much time together. When we do, our discussions are usually about politics, and hold the tension of distance between our ages. Larissa, my daughter, is in her early twenties, my mother is over eighty. When my mother and daughter speak about "the world" or "society" or "workers" or "human nature" or "commitment" or "responsibility," they do not mean the same things. Perhaps without me they would not know what the other intended to say. Larissa, after four years studying philosophy, is becoming a painter. My mother has been a committed political activist for almost sixty years.

Today, we find ourselves seated next to one another at a large dining room table. Larissa has just graduated from Harvard. A filmmaker has been conducting interviews with "red-diaper babies," the children of Socialist and Communist parents. He has invited the three of us to participate in his film about the way parents' political activities affect their children.

Projector lights are adjusted, the sound system is regulated, the filmmaker addresses me while my mother and daughter listen. I tell the story of the day my mother was arrested for advocating the "overthrow of the government by force and violence in 1951." It is an old story, by now written and published in a book about my mother's life. I don't expect it to carry any urgency. Nevertheless, when I arrive at the moment of my mother's arrest, which took place early one morning when I was still asleep, I feel a sharp clutching at my throat, as if some internal monitor still thought it necessary to keep me from crying. I have since looked at the footage of this interview, impressed by the seamless delivery of the story that moves steadily across my lips as if it provoked no inner drama.

Now it is my daughter's turn. I've been curious about her willingness to participate in this interview. What in the world would she say? At that time I still thought of myself as my mother's daughter; I had not fully grasped my identity as my daughter's mother. I had no idea that I was just about to become the subject of her mother-stories. In front of the camera, the lights tilted in her direction, the microphone pinned to her lapel, my daughter is reflecting on the tendency to repeat patterns over the generations.

"I just realized it the other week, how much my mother . . . I mean, she didn't really mean to . . . it's very hard for me to talk about this . . ." Larissa hesitates, then begins again. "I think she made me relive the feelings she had as a little girl. When I was little, six years old, she left me for about six weeks in Ireland. I was staying with some friends. I was taking a nap and when I woke up I asked where she was and she was gone. She was just gone. She hadn't woken me up to say good-bye. I always remembered that. When I was eight years old I stayed with my father and stepmother. She went away to Israel for nine months. She went away and she left me. It makes me very sad and also very angry. . . . Those were the hardest things in my life to deal with. . . . That's what was passed down from my mother's childhood to mine, but it was not about politics, it was just that pattern. . . ."

Her need to tell this story must be very great. She has never told it before and now she is telling it in public, before a camera. We are all impressed with the way the story rises under an enormous interior pressure and keeps coming, through tears and embarrassment. She is smoking a cigarette; she looks down frequently at her hands, then straight at me, making sure that I am taking all this in. My mother, on my left, seems afraid that any moment now the Chernin women will lose it entirely in front of the camera and disgrace ourselves in public. She clutches my hand, warning me perhaps to stop Larissa. But I know better. This is a tense, true, wrenching moment of confrontation and we will all survive it. My daughter, who has always been protective of me, has just told her first mother-story full of blame and reproach and anger and recrimination. There are going to be rocky years ahead, filled with stories and their revisions.

Later, it occurs to me that I have never, ever directly told my own mother how much I suffered when she was taken away to jail. My stories have always been tales of a proud, untroubled, courageous daughter. I have stayed true to my childhood mission not to make life harder for my mother by letting her know my anguish. My mother (as the storytellers say) will go to her grave without hearing me speak a single word of blame or reproach; a lonely space of the untold story will always stand between us. My daughter, by contrast, has just asked me to face the truth of the way I mothered her.

Stories breed stories, as we know. Sometimes, even the untold stories get through. Or maybe my mother listened to Larissa's story of her childhood as if I had been talking about my own. Perhaps, watching us together, she understood that one could face the truth about oneself as a mother. Several months later, when I was visiting her in Los Angeles, the same filmmaker showed up to interview us again. On that occasion, sitting in the library of the retirement home in which my mother was then living, we began to talk about the difficult years of her arrest, incarceration and trial as a Communist. It was once again a public occasion, with cameras and lights and microphones pinned to our lapels. Suddenly, in the midst of all this, my mother says she knew her life as a political activist had troubled her young daughter.

"So here is maybe something I didn't say before . . . didn't say, not to myself, not to my daughter. . . . If she was asleep in bed when I came home late from a meeting, I tried to tell myself, so, she is a young girl, she needs her sleep. If she is asleep, how could she miss her mother? Sometimes I would bring her something to eat, some cake or cookies left over from the meeting. Then I would tell myself, she's a young girl, she needs her sleep, why do you wake her? But the feeling was always there, an anguish, this child growing up with the mother always away from the home, always out in the world, always busy . . . sometimes it was so hard to go on with the work, so hard, knowing the child is at home, missing the mother . . ."

My mother, a tough, seasoned, woman, is crying in public over the suffering she caused her child. The camera moves in on her face, with its deep furrows and luminous eyes, and does not move away while this confession, held back all these years between us, finally takes place, collapsing our solitary, lifelong alienation from one another.

I imagine that was the day I began to appreciate the power of storytelling to change lives. I had already written about my mother's life, taken over and invented her voice. I wrote the book at a time when I was struggling to forgive my mother for the wrongs of my childhood. I was not ready yet to let go of her, certainly not to give birth to her. The book gave birth to a new relationship between us, a collaboration that broke down frequently over the years as we fell back into our exasperated inability to tolerate our temperamental differences. I had created a narrative mother, whom we both subsequently adopted, the real mother for the rest of her life telling her stories as I had told them. Then, one day, during an intimate public moment, my mother tells me that she knew how I suffered as a child. Suddenly, I am thrust forward into a flurry of emotion that leaves me aware, when it subsides, that I now have a new version of our story. The past, stretched taut by then and clearly at its breaking point, lets us go. I realize there is nothing to blame her for, nothing to forgive; we were never a great match as mother and daughter but we came through.

For the last years of her life I experienced a tenderness for her that introduced into our relationship the first extended mothering that ever freely entered it. Nine years after Larissa's graduation I gave birth to myself as my mother's mother. Our lives together completed themselves in a gesture that wrapped us up and closed our bond. I lift her up in my arms, this once powerful woman now frail and emaciated on the day before she dies, to hold her passionately, singing to her, rocking her, against my breast.

Two years after my mother's death, Larissa and I are at the Japanese tea pavilion in Golden Gate Park. I have invited her to meet me here so that she could tell me stories about her childhood. We keep postponing the moment, although we both think her stories would find a place in my collection. We are in a lighthearted mood and neither of us wants to take on troubling business. Still, we have grown up to be disciplined women, we have agreed to undertake this project and we will get to it. I have brought the tape recorder, we've chosen a quiet corner where we can talk. Meanwhile, we have been bent over the fish pond, leaning shoulder to shoulder on the wooden chairs without backs, sipping tea from tiny cups. As soon as either one of us looks away for a moment, the other steals an almond cookie from her plate. This is an old game, which we have played in this tea garden since she was a little girl.

Many years ago, when she was first leaving home to attend college, she used to tell stories about the way we always went to the park after school. Her memory of that time was clear and vivid, textured with sensual detail and no doubt highly idealized. Later, when she'd been away from home for a few years, she stopped telling these stories; in fact, she seemed to have forgotten entirely about the late afternoons we had spent in the tea garden. She retained almost nothing, she said, from her childhood except bleakness, grayness and depression.

"Suppose," I say, picking up another game, "I paid for your tea and cookies and gave the waitress one dollar. How much change would I get?"

"You paid for my tea and cookies? Then, I would get back two quarters, a dime and a penny. Or maybe, five nickels, a quarter, and eleven pennies. Except that you wouldn't want all those pennies would you? Unless we were going to throw them into the pond for wishes. But I hope you remember this time not to scare the goldfish. Or we might get back six dimes and a penny. But if you were paying for your own tea too, the waitress would give us a quarter, a dime and a nickel and a penny, and you'd leave the dime and nickel for her tip."

This had been the correct answer twenty-five years earlier, when the daughter was six or seven years old, good at math and liked to tease her mother, who wasn't. Back then the tea (which now costs over two dollars a serving) had been not much more than a quarter for cookies and teapot and tiny cup. A lot of cookies could be wasted feeding the birds, bluejays and pigeons that hopped about the stone temples on the tiny islands in the goldfish pond. Sometimes they flew over and settled on the wooden tables, although the waitress disapproved and shooed them away, particularly during the cherry tree season when the garden was filled with tourists. In those days, the daughter admired the mother for not being intimidated by the waitresses. Even when other mothers and daughters had given in and left off feeding the birds, the two of us went right on sprinkling crumbs on the table.

I sometimes tried, in the years after her graduation, to evoke these golden hours for Larissa, who shrugged them off. She was angry, and her stories told me how consistently I had let her down. It is true that I spent hours shut away in the small, dark room she called the "mole hole," where I wrote in my notebook, meditated, translated Rilke and Hölderlin and ignored my child. I didn't know yet how to listen to a daughter's stories. I tried to protect myself from them.

"I certainly loved you, I did the best I could. I was incredibly depressed. I tried to hide it from you."

"Why? Why didn't you just let me know?"

"Well, sometimes I did let you know. I told you I was going through a hard time and hoped you'd understand. . . ."

"You think I wanted to know my mother was going through a hard time?"

"Well, that's why I tried to keep it hidden. . . ."

"You call that trying? You really think you tried?"

I used to let Larissa walk by herself over the humped-back

bridge, where children under seven were not supposed to go alone, although some fathers let their boys go up there. Holding hands, we would embark on another forbidden pleasure to race across the slippery stones that led over the winding streams. We treated the garden like our own back yard; it was several blocks from where we lived, we came here daily after school to do math, feed the birds, risk the displeasure of the guardians of the garden. These are the stories about us I wish my daughter would tell, but she has something else in mind, she has assured me.

I am going to find out what my daughter now thinks of the way she was raised. She has moved back from the East Coast, she's a feminist, a risk-taking, well-educated woman, she has a black belt in tae kwon do, has worked as a bartender and a waitress, taken care of kids in an after-school neighborhood program, been to Europe, traveled about by herself, picked grapes, lived in Paris, speaks French fluently, moved back to San Francisco from Cambridge a few years ago, teaches art in a private school, grows her hair long then cuts it short and immediately starts growing it again, doesn't like to get dressed up when we go to the opera, is capable and virile and always cries, leaning in close to me, when Violetta dies at the end of *Traviata*. She is a painter and she does not want to have children. Is this because she knows she would be the same kind of mother her own mother was and does not wish to inflict that on a child?

"Why don't you tell me why you don't want to have children? Maybe we could begin that way. . . . I know it's hard to begin. I never managed to tell my mother the whole truth about anything."

"I don't mind telling you the truth. You never thought you were the greatest mother in the world, did you?" she asks in her pointed, playful way.

"I never thought I was the world's greatest mother. But I also never knew how to think about it from your point of view."

"Typical," she says, glancing at me from the corner of her eye. This is another of the games we have learned to play, telling the hard truth as if telling it came easily and the hardness no longer mattered.

"Did you say typical?"

"You wanted the truth, didn't you?" Then, afraid she might have played too rough, she takes my arm and leans up hard against my shoulder. "Didn't you?"

"Okay," I say, finding this harder than I imagined, "I'm listening."

"Why I don't want to have children? I think I would feel so horribly responsible for the little creature's well-being. So identified with its need, you know? I'd be constantly worrying, suffering for it, imagining it might be needing me. I wouldn't be free to think about my own needs and wants. Then I'd get angry at it for being such a helpless creature and I'd have to pay more attention to make up for being angry. Anyway, I feel that I am leaving something behind in my paintings, I don't need continuity through a child. And well, this isn't so easy to say," she adds in rush, "but if you want the truth . . . I'm afraid I'd be like you, moody, unable to control your temper—that's scary for a little kid, it really is . . ."

We leave the tea garden, cross the street and enter the arboretum, another place we visited regularly when she was little. Recently, she has begun to paint scenes from this garden with a radiant palate that evokes a fecund, teeming, overgrown luxuriance. I recognize in her paintings places we knew over twenty-five years ago and always name them correctly. Today, wandering through them, we are caught between the past and her re-creation

213

of it, identifying the garden by invoking the paintings she has made of it, from memory, twenty-five years later.

"Are you okay, Mom?" she asks. There is the anguish I used to see on her face when she was a little girl trying hard to take good care of me. "I mean, I didn't come out here to hurt your feelings . . ."

"I like it when we tell the truth. I've always liked it. And this truth," I say, kissing the top of her head, "is not exactly new between us."

"The trouble is," she says, as we step out on a little wooden pier from one of her paintings, "I've told you everything I remember." She says this thoughtfully, frowning at her hands and scraping the cuticle of her left thumb. She does this whenever we move out of our bantering mode. "Honestly, it doesn't mean all that much to me anymore. I used to want to tell these stories to anyone who would listen. I was angry at you and I wanted you to hear them. But now . . . I think I have probably worn them out. I'm done with them, there's not much in them anymore."

"Are we avoiding something?" I ask, wondering if perhaps we should.

She takes hold of my hand as we lean far down over the water. "I don't think so. I really don't think so." I note the firm grasp of her fine, capable hand, holding me back when I seem to be falling forward. She means what she says. She is not resisting my invitation to talk. "We've done it already. We have, Mom. The truth is, I don't have anything more to say. You probably know my stories better than I do. Why don't you just go ahead and tell them?"

She's laughing, one of those secret laughs meaningful only to a mother and daughter.

"Really? You'd let me? Take over your stories?"

"Sure, go ahead," she says, with an exaggerated resignation, "you would anyway, wouldn't you? Just like you did with Grandma's stories? And I, really, really, I just don't seem to care about them anymore. Maybe you should tell how we finally got done with those stories and don't have anything more to say about them. It happens, doesn't it? Don't people finally get tired of repeating these things?"

"Not in our family . . . no, somehow I didn't think that would happen with us."

"So that's where we are . . . you can write about that. . . . You can say what a relief it is. Don't you think so?" She is excited by this unexpected reversal of our plans to spend the afternoon telling stories. She's walking faster, still holding my hand, pulling me along behind her. When she looks back at me, I can see how proud she is of altering, single-handedly, the family pattern.

She's letting go, I tell myself, she's letting go of the stories. This makes me, as a mother, very happy for her. As a collector of mother-stories I am forced to realize once again how these prized and cherished stories, having served their purpose, finally must be put to rest for a time. Perhaps I will never hear again about the way, when she came home from school as a little girl, she would find me sitting in my dark downstairs room listening to opera with earphones, singing along, off-key, repeating, not quite under my breath, Elektra's desperate cry to Agamemnon. Perhaps she has already forgotten the way I healed our dog Elisabeth's ears by putting my hands over them and praying. The dog, who had been whimpering and whining and casting baleful glances at us, grew absolutely still, rested quietly with her head between my hands, barked once, softly, and was suddenly, wondrously, free from pain. Larissa used to like to tell how Elisabeth followed me about for the

215

rest of that evening, never more than an inch from my side, care-fully lowering herself beside me to rest her muzzle on my feet. I will miss even the difficult stories, about the way I left her in Ire-land without waking her to say good-bye. The way I wrapped her sandwiches in used plastic bags before the days of recycling had begun, causing serious embarrassment for her at lunchtime. I will miss the good story, our best story, about the tea parties we had in my little room, the two of us inventing a nonsense language we called Sneesnaw as we toasted each other with tiny doll-size cups. Does she still even remember how to talk Sneesnaw?

We've been moving through twenty-five years of our relation-ship together since we entered the park, walking about as if we were figures in her drawings and paintings, our shared past trans-posed into her visionary recollection of childhood. She has just let go of her childhood stories, or maybe they have let go of her. I now have to release my claim to them. I can't ask her to retell them. I can't gather them in to pin them to my collection. This is her moment, it marks a distinct stage in her development; she is leaving the stories behind; tactfully, appropriately, she is separat-ing herself from my interests. I have no right to tamper with this movement. I can only hold my breath, trusting the stories will someday find their way back into the telling.

Mother-stories, because they are lived as they are old, then told again in order to relive them, belong to the category of stories that can never end. Mother-stories may fall silent for a time as the daughter moves out into her maturity. It makes no difference. Sooner or later, I have observed, the mother-stories will crop up again, pressing for renewal and revision. A mother dies, the story of her life and her relationship to her daughter is resurrected. This is now the mourning-story, a tale with a black border around the edges, and it will do what it can to see the daughter through. The story has become, along with all other purposes it has served, memory's chapel. It is visited with circumspection. The harsh episodes soften, the longing to idealize returns, repetitions make their way back in, along with the evolving tale of the daughter's loss. Now the grandchild gets involved. Her own mother's grief over the loss of her mother impresses the little girl. She gets interested in her grandmother for the first time. "What was your mother's name?" she asks, and then without waiting for an answer, "Hey, what was your father's name?" She is a child of Berkeley and the late nineties and is surprised to discover that her grandmother and grandfather, Padrick and Shiovan Kelly, both had the same last name. Her parents, both lawyers, have kept their professional names when they married. Their daughter carries both names, which makes her last name different from either of theirs and this is the way it seems to her it should be. The strange fact that grandmother and grandfather had the same last name causes the story to be carried to school, where it turns out that not many kids know the name of their grandparents, but most find it definitely weird that their grandparents too might have shared a name.

What can it possibly mean?

This question now comes to preoccupy the little girl, who wants to know about her mother's mother and how she happened to give up her own name when she married her husband. The story of this woman who lost her name has not greatly interested the child's mother for many years. Now, however, in answer to her daughter's questions, she fetches some old photograph albums and the little five-year-old immediately points out, from among the identical, old, faded black-and-white prints, which of the plump women with ample bosoms was her grandmother. She has developed an attachment to the strange lady and puzzles deeply about the fact that the grandmother was once young, had a mother of her own, grew up, gave birth to the mother of the child who is asking the questions. But when all is said and done she still finds it very strange that she had two grandparents, both of whom had the same last name.

This small detail, inconspicuous and irrelevant a generation earlier, has now launched a young girl's interest in mothers and daughters and may be the first element in her own future mother-story. Maybe she will draw a picture of the older woman and put it up on the refrigerator. Or the story may sink down into her to be lost for many years before it returns to mark a stage in her development.

A few years ago Larissa painted a portrait of our relationship. Did it, I wonder, prepare for this moment of letting go? Someone else might read this painting differently. My daughter herself might have had something else in mind. I, eager to bring my collection to a legitimate close, may have to end where I began, with interpretation.

There is a woman in a long granny dress, of the type I wore frequently during the seventies. The woman is followed by a blond little girl with curly hair, a self-portrait of my daughter. The two walk through a vibrant patch of yellow, perhaps a field of wheat or rye. The mother and child come from the left, from out of the past, with steady determination, beneath a sky that shows a small yellow ball of sun next to a large yellow sickle moon. This is a landscape in which opposites have been brought together. Work that leads to wholeness is underway. Together, the mother and child walk toward a mysterious blue house with a red roof. It dominates the foreground of their painted world and draws them toward it.

I used this painting for the cover of my book about my mother. To describe it accurately I look behind me at the far wall of my office. There, I have displayed this portrait through which (in my interpretation) my daughter left behind all earlier stories, their protection and blame, their separation and anguish and loss, to portray the two of us in a new relationship.

Yes, there we are, serenely on our way through luminous thickets of paint toward our house of transformations.

Once there, who can say what will happen between us?

Is this a house where a birth will take place?